WHAT PEOPLE ARE SAYING...

Sonship: The Mantle, The Journey, The Double Portion by my friend, Joshua Gay, is an absolute must read for all leaders in ministry, and those preparing for ministry. This powerfully anointed book is a strategic manual that is sure to have a worldwide impact. Amazing!

—**PASTOR JUDY JACOBS**
DWELLING PLACE CHURCH INTERNATIONAL, CLEVELAND TN
AUTHOR & WORSHIP LEADER

In this book, Joshua Gay outlines not only the principle, but also the praxis of sonship. He teaches us, not only how to think, but also how to act as sons and daughters. Without an understanding of what Joshua has captured in these pages, our impact for the kingdom will be highly limited, and our journey in discipleship will be riddled with challenges.

—**MICAH WOOD**
DIRECTOR OF STRATEGY, THE RAMP & AUTHOR

This is a kingdom message for the church. God's desire is to pass revival down to each generation—from fathers to sons and from mothers to daughters. We must all heed the word of *Sonship*, or risk missing what God wants to do in this hour. The principles that Joshua Gay outlines in each chapter will transform your life.

—**KAREN WHEATON**
FOUNDER & SENIOR LEADER, THE RAMP

Sonship is a scripturally rich, personally inspiring and powerfully motivating book. The principles that Joshua Gay outlines in this book create a practical pathway towards receiving the double portion anointing that makes generational continuity possible.

—**PASTOR JANE HAMON**
VISION CHURCH, SANTA ROSA FL
AUTHOR

In *Sonship*, Joshua Gay has captured all the salient points that a good spiritual son needs in order to be successful in the kingdom of God. By reading this book you will receive an impartation to move and walk in sonship in obedience to God's Word and His law.

—**PASTOR JAY MCKESEY**
NEW VISION CHRISTIAN CENTER INTERNATIONAL, LONGWOOD FL

SONSHIP

JOSHUA GAY

Parsons Publishing House
Your Voice Your World ™

Sonship: The Mantle. The Journey. The Double Portion.
by Joshua Gay

Parsons Publishing House
P. O. Box 488
Stafford, VA 22554 USA
www.ParsonsPublishingHouse.com
Info@ParsonsPublishingHouse.com

All Scripture quotations, unless otherwise indicated, are taken from the *New King James Version*® (NKJV). Copyright © 1982 by Thomas Nelson, Inc. Used by permission. All rights reserved.

Scripture quotations marked "The Amplified Bible" or "The Amplified New Testament" are taken from The Amplified Bible, Old Testament copyright 1965, 1987 by the Zondervan Corporation and The Amplified New Testament copyright 1958, 1987 by The Lockman Foundation. Used by permission. All rights reserved.

Publisher's Note: Disregarding English grammar rules, Publisher has opted to reference satan and related names with lowercase letters.

Cover Art: Micah Gay
Photography: Kaydee Albritton

ISBN-13: 978-1602730526
ISBN-10: 1602730520
Library of Congress Control Number: 2014908843
Printed in the United States of America.
For World-Wide Distribution.

ACKNOWLEDGMENTS

I would like to thank the wonderful people who have been such a blessing during the process of writing this book.

First of all, I want to thank my wife, Miranda. You are the greatest blessing to my life. Your words and actions continually encourage me to go after everything God has for me. You are my greatest supporter and source of strength. Thank you for everything that you have done to make this book possible. Thank you for standing by my side and being the greatest wife anyone could ask for. I love you more than any words can express.

I also want to thank my two children: Josiah and Hannalee. Daddy is so proud of you. Even at a young age, I can see the abundant love that you have for Jesus and your entire family. I am so blessed and honored that Father God entrusted your mother and I with the privilege of stewarding over your lives. Daddy loves you.

I want to thank my parents, Robert and Stacey Gay. Thank you can barely begin to express my gratitude for everything you have done in my life. You have been, and continue to be, an incredible example of a godly marriage and ministry. Thank you for not simply being great ministers, but more importantly, great parents. Thank you for training me up in the fear and admonition of the Lord. Thank you for recognizing what God placed inside of me and placing a demand on it. I can't say thank you enough. I love you.

I would like to acknowledge my siblings, Micah and Kayla, and their spouses, Chelsea and Kelvin. You are not simply family, you are some of my closest friends. Your support during the writing of this book has been invaluable. It is an honor to serve the Lord and the Church alongside you. I couldn't ask for better siblings and friends. You guys are awesome.

Lastly, I would like to thank our High Praise Worship Center family. You guys are incredible. I frequently say that a church is nothing if not a family; I count each and every member of High Praise Worship Center as family. To every congregation member and leader, I treasure each and every one you more than words can express. Your relationship and support mean the world to me. I believe with all of my heart that God sent us the best people in the entire world to be a part of our assembly of believers. Thank you for providing a spiritual environment where the message of this book could be preached, practiced, and proven. Thank you for all the words of encouragement you have offered during this process. Thank you so much; I love you all.

FOREWORD

This book needs to be read by every person who wants to be a true son or father according to God's order. I will highly recommend this book to pastors who are trying to raise up spiritual sons in the faith. There are many Kingdom principles that will help, especially those who are desirous to fulfill spiritual ministry. Every Bible college student needs to have these truths incorporated into their lives. It will give them a better chance of fulfilling their calling and destiny in Christ Jesus.

I was impressed with the wisdom and maturity of a young pastor not yet in his thirties. Joshua has learned much and is to be commended for allowing the Lord to train and mature him beyond his years in life and ministry. I can verify that the truths and principles that Joshua presents are biblical and true to the realities of life.

During my sixty years of ministry I have witnessed and watched many young ministers with much potential to become great ministers for God. But so many did not practice the principles that Joshua presents in this book. They were called and had great zeal, but did not have spiritual fathers to mentor them, or they forsook their spiritual fathers and failed to fulfill their destiny.

The biblical characters and illustrations Joshua uses helps to make the truths understandable and applicable. I intend to give a copy to all my grandsons and grand-daughters. As Bishop to more than three thousand ministers, I will highly recommend that they read this book and give a copy to each of their children, both natural and spiritual sons and daughters.

Joshua, as your extended Bishop through your father, I am proud of the way you have allowed the Lord Jesus to mold you into a good model of true sonship. This will be only the first of many books you will write during your lifetime of ministry in the Lord Jesus Christ. May you and all who read this book practice these principles until you become the Third Reformation Reformers with the Joshua generation warrior anointing possessing the Promised Land, fulfilling all things, and bringing back Jesus the King of Kings ruling over everything.

Dr. Bill Hamon
Founder, Christian International Ministries
Santa Rosa, Florida

TABLE OF CONTENTS

Behold, I will send you Elijah the prophet before the coming of the great and dreadful day of the Lord. And he will turn the hearts of the fathers to the children, And the hearts of the children to their fathers..."

- Malachi 4:5-6 (NKJV)

PREFACE

One important thing we need in the Church today is an understanding of generations. We need an understanding of fathers and sons operating together for the purposes of the kingdom of God. God did not reveal Himself as the God of a single generation. Father God repeatedly revealed Himself as the "God of Abraham, the God of Isaac, and the God of Jacob." Why not simply the God of Abraham? Why not simply the God of David? Why not simply the God of Jehoshaphat, or any other significant man of faith in the Word of God? God continually reveals to us that He is a God of generations. God is interested in sons and daughters. He is concerned about generations.

The Bible has a tremendous amount to say about sons and daughters. The Prophet Joel declared that our "SONS and DAUGHTERS will prophesy" (Joel 2:28-33). Malachi prophesied that before the coming of the great and dreadful day of the Lord that hearts of the fathers would be turned to their children, and the hearts of the children to their fathers (Malachi 4:5-6). The psalmist said that children, sons and daughters, are a heritage from the Lord (Psalm 127:3). God is interested in fathers and sons—mothers and daughters. God is focused on multi-generational ministry arising in the earth.

In the process of writing this book, a true General in the Church, Steve Hill, received his eternal reward. Steve Hill was the primary evangelist and speaker during the Brownsville Revival in Pensacola, Florida. If you are unfamiliar with this move of God, the outpouring lasted for over five years, and as a result of it over 200,000 souls came to know Christ. Whether you agree or disagree with the revival, you cannot argue with that kind of fruit. Steve Hill was the primary voice God used to bring people to the saving knowledge of His Son during this time period.

On March 14th, 2014, I sat watching the memorial service for Steve Hill in my living room. Despite never having had the privilege of meeting Steve Hill, nor attending the Brownsville Revival, I found myself becoming emotional. The Body of Christ had lost a great man of God. The service was beautiful, a remembrance of Steve as a father, husband, and minister of the Gospel.

John Kilpatrick, who was pastor of Brownsville Assembly of God during the outpouring, ministered the message that night. I sat and listened to Pastor Kilpatrick remember his friend and co-laborer. My ears perked up when he began to speak of the mentors that both he and Steve had served under. Pastor Kilpatrick and Steve Hill both embraced the mantle of sonship. Steve had been mentored under two great men of God: David Wilkerson and Leonard Ravenhill. Steve actually called these men his "spiritual fathers." Pastor Kilpatrick said of Steve Hill that he was a "different man" and "something was on him" after the death of Leonard Ravenhill. Could it be that Steve Hill had received a double portion of the anointing that Leonard Ravenhill operated in?

Pastor Kilpatrick stated that one of the reasons that the revival in Pensacola "worked" was due to the fact that both he and Steve Hill understood SPIRITUAL AUTHORITY. He went on to say that because Steve Hill understood spiritual authority, "God entrusted him." God entrusts the stewardship of the spirit of revival to proven and faithful sons.

The revival that happened in Brownsville wasn't something that God desired to only do in that place. I don't believe what God entrusted to Steve Hill was something only for him, but rather for faithful sons. Revival, restoration, and reformation are something God wants to do everywhere. God wants to move in your life, in your city, and in your church. He wants revival in churches all over America and the entire world. This will happen when the hearts of the fathers are turned to the sons, and sons to the fathers (Malachi 4:5-6).

I believe that the hearts of fathers have already turned. Just in the last couple of years I have heard so many Generals in the faith begin to talk about God turning their hearts toward sons and daughters, toward a generation that is arising in the earth today. However, the prophecy of Malachi doesn't stop with the hearts of fathers turning, but continues to sons turning unto fathers. As father's hearts are turned to us, we must embrace sonship and turn to them. It is not a one-way street.

Elisha operated under a double portion mantle because he was willing to undergo the process of sonship. A double portion anointing, a spirit of revival, is still released upon faithful sons and daughters. When we are humble, promotion and anointing come as a secondary consequence.

I want to see God pour out His spirit in an unprecedented way. I want to see the Church in the world today be a reflection of the Church in the book of Acts, but with even more miracles, authority, and power! We will see later in this book that this is the way God designed for His Church to work. Anointing is meant to increase not to decrease. This all happens when we EMBRACE the mantle of sonship! If we embrace sonship, future generations will operate in greater levels of spiritual power and anointing.

What does the mantle really mean? What does the life of sonship look like? What is the double portion journey? Let's find out. Embark on the journey of *Sonship: The Mantle. The Journey. The Double Portion.* and see your life and the entire world changed for His glory.

CHAPTER 1
FATHERS, YOUNG MEN AND LITTLE CHILDREN

I write to you, little children, Because your sins are forgiven you for His name's sake. I write to you, fathers, Because you have known Him who is from the beginning. I write to you, young men, Because you have overcome the wicked one. I write to you, little children, Because you have known the Father. I have written to you, fathers, Because you have known Him who is from the beginning. I have written to you, young men, Because you are strong, and the word of God abides in you, And you have overcome the wicked one.

These things I have written to you who believe in the name of the Son of God, that you may know that you have eternal life, and that you may continue to believe in the name of the Son of God (1 John 2:12-14, 5:13).

In this passage of Scripture, John is attempting to communicate something of great importance. To understand the significance of what he is stating, we must first understand the demographic of whom John is addressing. We see very clearly that John is writing to believers—to those

1

who call Jesus Lord. He says that he is writing to those "who believe in the Son of God" and encouraging them to "continue to believe." You can only continue if you have already started. Whereas the Gospel of John was written primarily to the unbeliever to testify of the works Jesus, John's epistles were written to challenge, exhort, and identify the body of Christ.

This is exactly what John is doing in the previous passage of Scripture; he's identifying those in the Church. He identifies three types of believers: little children, young men, and fathers. All believers fall into one of these three classifications. These stages of maturity are not determined by age, sex, race, or even education. None of these things are relevant to that which John is referring. He is talking about spiritual maturity. John is talking about spiritual development.

Some have stated that John was identifying people by a natural age; however, I don't believe this to be so. If we believe that, we must also believe that John is specifically speaking only to those who are naturally young when he says "little children." John was not identifying believers based on chronological age. He implores "little children" to stay away from idols. Is this something he is only stating to those of younger age? Of course not. All people are to stay away from idols. However, this is something imperative for those young in the faith to learn. This is a truth of great importance that is being enunciated to those who are babes in Christ.

John is stating elementary principles that need to be known and practiced in order to see spiritual maturity realized. He starts in the same place God started with the Ten Commandments. Commandment one is, "You shall have no other gods before Me" (Exodus 20:3). Before you can progress in maturity you must first understand that God comes first. If God is first, there will be no idols. He must be the priority. This was the first commandment in the Ten Commandments for a reason. It is an elementary and foundational principle. This is an introductory idea that needs to be understood by young believers.

The Natural and the Spiritual

We must understand that God does nothing by accident. He is intentional in everything He initiates, creates, and establishes. John, inspired by the Holy Spirit, specifically uses the maturation process of natural things to show us something in the spiritual realm. In this case, it is the progression of spiritual maturity. As it is in the natural realm, so it is in the spiritual realm.

We see many spiritual principles that are mirrored in the natural realm. Likewise, there are many natural principles that are mirrored in the spiritual realm. The principle of sowing and reaping is one of these principles. Similarly, we see the principle of spiritual maturity mirrored in natural maturity. Let's take a look at the spiritual progression of maturity and these three categories of believers that John specifically mentions.

Little Children

John begins by addressing "little children." This is important because it is the starting point in a process of maturity. No one is born a teenager or as a fully matured adult. Everyone starts as a little child—as a baby. We have often used the term "spiritual babes" in church culture to identify those who are new to the faith. John is comparatively identifying those who are young in the faith.

A spiritual baby is someone who has believed on Jesus as their Lord and accepted Him as Savior. They have experienced the new birth. John reinforces that idea when he declares the reason he writes to them is because their "sins are forgiven." This marks the beginning of a process, a starting point of a spiritual journey. When anyone makes Jesus the Lord of their life by accepting His redemptive work at Calvary, they are born again. This is the new birth, a new start, a new beginning for one's life. They become a new creation in Christ Jesus (2 Corinthians 5:17).

Far too many people have made salvation the end of the spiritual journey. They have made it the end of the spiritual maturation process in the life of a believer. God never designed this to be the end of the process. Could you imagine if a baby was born and always remained a baby? It is ludicrous to even imagine a twenty-five year old walking around in a diaper with a bottle in their mouth. However, that is exactly what we propagate when we view salvation as the end of the journey. They are saying that the process of spiritual maturity ends when one is still in spiritual diapers and only drinking milk.

Salvation through the redemptive work of Jesus is a truth that we should know in its fullness, but it is not the only truth contained in the Word of God. All other truths hinge on this revelation, just as everything you learn naturally hinges on you being born into this world. You cannot learn if you do not exist. You also cannot mature spiritually until you are born again.

In the natural, you can't drive an automobile until you come to a certain level of maturity. You can't run until you first walk, you can't walk until you first crawl, and you can't crawl without being born. In the spiritual realm, you can't have a revelation of God as *Jehovah Jireh*, the God who provides, without first having a revelation of Him as your Savior and Redeemer. Everything is BUILT upon that understanding. However, it is not the end! Rather, it is the foundation from which everything else flows and grows. Your spiritual maturity was never meant to culminate at salvation. It begins there.

The experience of a child being born into the world is both wonderful and exciting. Many hearts are filled with emotion and joy as a new child is welcomed into a family and home. As a result, from that point on, there is a celebration every year on that day. In our culture today, we celebrate the day that we were born. We have parties and receive gifts to commemorate and remember that day as we grow older.

However, as wonderful as it was when one was born into this world and welcomed into a family, we do not expect them to still be in diapers with a bottle in their mouth at their twenty-fifth birthday celebration. This would be considered dysfunctional and there would be a valid reason to question their maturity and progression in life. If this were the case, they would possibly be evaluated by psychologists and doctors to diagnose the issue.

So why should anyone think it is acceptable if we do not mature spiritually? Should it be considered permissible for someone to remain in the same spiritual state as the day they were saved? Should we not mature as we get older in our walk with God? Of course we should! Is this an unrealistic expectation? I don't believe so.

Parents expect their children to mature as they get older. Is this an unreasonable request from parents? It is most certainly not! Natural maturity is a normal aspect of the life progression of a healthy well-adjusted human being. Likewise, I believe God expects us to mature as we "get older" in the faith. As a healthy well-adjusted believer, we should mature spiritually. Maturity is expected.

My wife and I have two wonderful children. They are a blessing to our lives. We have a son named Josiah who was born in 2009 and a daughter named Hannalee who was born in 2012. They are both a joy to our lives. It was cute when our babies played. When they made silly faces it was cute. When they learned to walk it was cute. It was even cute when they made a mess. Every parent understands to what I'm referring. Every young child has done something undesirable and made a mess; yet, even in the midst of the mess they were still cute and adorable.

I can remember a specific moment when Josiah was in his highchair eating spaghetti (or "basgetti" as he called it at the time). He was focused on his food and immersed in his eating to such a degree that he hardly lifted his head. When he finally finished and looked up, it seemed there was more spaghetti sauce on his face than went into his mouth. He looked at me and smiled with the biggest grin, and it was adorable.

Josiah is now older. It is no longer cute if he makes a mess with food all over his face at mealtime. Why? It is because he is no longer a baby! There is a greater expectation as he matures. It is not unreasonable nor am I being difficult to expect more from him. It's very simple: as he gets older and matures, the messy consumption of food becomes unacceptable. In the same manner, that which was acceptable when you were either a spiritual babe or little child comes to a place of unacceptability as you get older.

Young believers are going to mess up. They are going to make mistakes, as we all do. Thank God for His mercy when we make a mess. However, you were never intended to live in a continual mess. There are far too many believers who are still in spiritual diapers with spaghetti all over their faces because they have refused to mature spiritually. They would rather have milk than meat. There are some behaviors that may be acceptable whenever one is a new Christian; however, one is expected to grow up and mature. No one was ever intended to stay a spiritual baby.

I recognize that everyone has to start somewhere. No one is born into maturity. However, you were never meant to live in a perpetual state of immaturity. Think about this. In the natural realm, your time as a baby is a VERY small percentage of your life. You weren't meant to stay a baby for long. It is time to progress and grow up in the things of God. It is time to stop getting food all over your face; get out of diapers, pick up your fork, and eat the meat of the Word. Don't allow yourself to stay a spiritual baby. Choose to grow up!

Fathers

Next, John also addresses fathers. This is the last state of spiritual progression. He specifically states that fathers have

7

"known Him who is from the beginning." They don't simply know Him; they know Him from the BEGINNING.

The Greek word that John uses here for *beginning* denotes two distinct understandings. First, it denotes the fullness of a thing. Secondly, it denotes order. Fathers do not simply know God in one facet or in one dimension; they know God in His fullness. They know God in His complexity. Spiritual fathers know and respect God's order.

The Fullness of God

Understanding the fullness of God is attained in three primary ways: time, experience, and revelation knowledge. Children still have a lot to learn about the world. My children, if left to their own devices, would do things to hurt themselves. This is not because they want to hurt themselves. Rather, they lack experience to understand that you should not stick a fork in the electrical outlet. I, as a father, know that if I stick a fork in an electrical outlet that I will get electrocuted. Where did I get this information? I honestly can't remember an exact time when I learned this. It was simply something that I learned over time.

The spiritual realm functions in the same manner. There are some things that are learned over time. This comes from reading your Bible, being in prayer, attending church regularly, and simply experiencing time and being faithful with what time you've been given. Hebrews speaks of this.

Hebrews 5:14 says, "But solid food belongs to those who are of full age, *that is*, those who **by reason of use have their senses exercised** to discern both good and evil" (*emphasis added*).

Notice the phrase, "by reason of use have their senses exercised." This is knowledge that doesn't necessarily come from a specific moment, but rather is received over the course of being faithful to the Lord. This is one of the ways that fathers have gained knowledge and wisdom. They have simply been faithful over the course of time. Praise God for the faithfulness of spiritual fathers.

Experience is a way through which fathers have been able to fathom the full extent of God. Time will always lead to experience. The longer you serve the Lord; the more of Him you experience. The more faithful you are to Him over the course of time; the more experience you have to draw upon about Him.

In Philippians 3:10, Paul, a spiritual father, talks about "knowing Jesus in the power of His resurrection." The Greek word he uses here when he talks about "knowing" is *ginosko*. Our modern English definition for "knowing" someone is very different than what is being communicated here by the Apostle Paul. The word was actually a Jewish idiom that was used to describe an intimate relationship between a husband and wife. Any married person can tell you that there are things that you don't know about your spouse until after you are married. There is limited knowledge until there is an intimate relationship that is designed to be experienced inside of the marriage covenant. You may think you know a person when you first meet and begin dating; however, you really do not know them until you are intimate inside the marriage covenant.

The only way you learn these things is by experience. There are things you can only know about a person by being intimate with them. There are some things about God you can only learn from being intimate with Him—from communing with Him. To learn these things, you cannot merely "date" God. You must be willing to forsake all others and come into a place of covenant with Him. There must be intimate moments between you and the Lord.

When God made man and woman He put them together and told them to be intimate. We are the bride of Christ. If we believe that we are His bride, then we must be intimate with Him. Spiritual fathers know the Lord in an intimate way. They have been close to Him and walked with Him for a long time. There is time, there is experience, and there is intimacy. The mixture of intimacy and time produces knowledge that can only come through that combination.

The last way that spiritual fathers know God in His fullness is through revelation knowledge. Isaiah declared that God's ways are higher than our ways and His thoughts are higher and grander than our thoughts (Isaiah 55:9). The word "thoughts" in this passage of Scripture could be translated plans and purposes. In order to know God in His fullness, you have to know His heart, plans, and purposes. The only way to receive and understand the plans and purposes of God is for Him to release them through revelation knowledge. Revelation knowledge is that which the Holy Spirit unfolds and reveals to us. It can only come through Him.

God is far above rational thinking and thought. Though we can learn about His character and nature through the Bible, we still must have revelation knowledge to know Him. Paul even said that God confounds the wise. This is because the wise are simply trying to understand him through the process of natural knowledge. The only way to know Him is to position yourself to receive revelation knowledge; natural knowledge is not enough.

For the message of the cross is foolishness to those who are perishing, but to us who are being saved it is the power of God. For it is written: "I WILL DESTROY THE WISDOM OF THE WISE, AND BRING TO NOTHING THE UNDERSTANDING OF THE PRUDENT." Where is the wise? Where is the scribe? Where is the disputer of this age? Has not God made foolish the wisdom of this world? For since, in the wisdom of God, the world through wisdom did not know God, it pleased God through the foolishness of the message preached to save those who believe. For Jews request a sign, and Greeks seek after wisdom; but we preach Christ crucified, to the Jews a stumbling block and to the Greeks foolishness, but to those who are called, both Jews and Greeks, Christ the power of God and the wisdom of God. Because the foolishness of God is wiser than men, and the weakness of God is stronger than men (1 Corinthians 1:18-25, emphasis added).

In this passage of Scripture, Paul speaks about God's ways being wiser than men and their method of operation. God's methods can seem perplexing to human rationale. He says, "For the message of the cross is foolishness to those who are perishing, but to us who are being saved it is the power of God." What Paul is pointing out is that the way God operates seems perplexing and can even seem foolish to the natural mind. He says that God uses foolishness or the irrational in the way He does things.

This is the reason we must possess revelation knowledge. Earthly knowledge and natural knowledge are essentially inadequate in relationship to revelation knowledge of the Word. There are atheists who "know" the Bible, yet do not "know" the Bible. Why? It is because their knowledge is simply like that of the Greeks whom Paul mentions: they are only looking for earthly wisdom.

> "The secret to a successful society is education. If we can just give everybody a good education, then it must follow that the world will get better and better." –Socrates[1]

This was the point of view in ancient Greece: the solution to all the problems in the world comes through natural academic knowledge. Today, we in America have a similar viewpoint. However, this is not God's perspective. While it is good for us to be educated, I believe it is a greater priority to the Lord that we possess revelation knowledge. Academic education alone is not the solution. REVELATION KNOWLEDGE that comes from heaven is the answer to all the problems in our world today.

I believe that God is always releasing revelation knowledge. Heaven is always broadcasting it. Those who have become fathers in the church have shown themselves faithful to position themselves to receive revelation knowledge from heaven.

The Power of Order

Spiritual fathers understand the order of God. Because of this understanding, they are empowered to release godly order into the lives of young men, into the lives of spiritual sons and daughters. Let's take a look at the power of order.

James 3:16 says, "For where envy and self-seeking exist, confusion and every evil thing are there." The Greek word that is translated *confusion* in this passage of Scripture literally means "a state of disorder." Fathers in the faith understand that God is neither envious of his children nor self-seeking. Therefore, order is produced. Where there is envy and self exaltation, there is disorder. Likewise, spiritual fathers are not self-seeking because they understand the necessity of the implementation of God's order.

I have heard people accuse spiritual fathers of being controlling when they attempt to bring order. Nothing could be further from the truth. Order is the furthest thing from being selfish and controlling. Order does not keep sons held down. Neither does it keep them from progressing forward into ministry or destiny. Order enables sons to be lifted up. Order establishes a way and method for accomplishment. It provides opportunity for sons and daughters to fulfill destiny. The order of God always allows us to be lifted up. When spiritual fathers establish godly order it allows sons to be elevated.

In the American church, we've had it backward when we equate disorder with opportunity. A person being allowed to do whatever they want has been called opportunity. The reality is that disorder and anarchy do not produce opportunity. Any place where there is the absence of order is a place of chaos, nothing more and nothing less. Disorder will keep you from going to the next level and progressing in the things of God. That which many have called freedom is actually a spirit of lawlessness that leads to bondage.

There are many today who view order as bondage. Nothing could be further from the truth. Speed limits posted on roads and highways are there to produce order. Are speed limits bondage? No, they are order. Is order bondage? Certainly not. Without order people get hurt! If there were no speed limits, many would drive at an unreasonable speed causing others to be hurt and killed because of the absence of order. There are many people who are asking for the spiritual "speed limit" (the order) to be removed. Where there is no order people get hurt and there is no blessing or manifestation of His glory.

In Exodus 25, we read where God gave Moses instructions on building the tabernacle. God did not tell Moses, "Build anything you want; just whatever you can dream up." No, He gave VERY specific instructions. God told him the type of wood, types of fabrics, and different types of animal hairs that were to be used. Was this because God was a control freak? No! The reason for this is very plain to see. In order for God's glory to dwell in a place, the vessel had to be fashioned according to the plan of God; according to His order. Things must be built according to the order of the Father because THE GLORY OF GOD WILL ALWAYS FOLLOW ORDER!

I believe that fathers have a proper understanding of God's order. Spiritual fathers help us establish order in our own lives so that we can be vessels full of glory. Like the Heavenly Father, true spiritual fathers in the church have an attitude that is not self-seeking or prideful and thus they operate and function in proper order. This order allows all to grow and be elevated to new levels of maturity, growth, and glory.

The Effects of Fatherlessness

I have heard so many people ask why spiritual fathers are important. To me, the answer is simple. When sons and daughters don't have fathers it negatively affects them. Let's look at some natural statistics on children who grow up without a natural father.

- 63% of youth suicides take place in fatherless homes—5 times the average.
- 90% of all homeless and runaway children are from fatherless homes—32 times the average.
- 85% of all children who show behavioral disorders come from fatherless homes—20 times the average.
- 80% of rapists with anger problems come from fatherless homes—14 times the average.
- 71% of all high school dropouts come from fatherless homes—9 times the average.[2]

The statistics are staggering when it comes to disorder and rebellion with its direct link to fatherlessness. Fathers bring order and are empowered to thwart self-destructive behavior and conduct. In the same manner, the opposite is true. The absence of fathers will produce disorder and destruction.

I have heard people say, "I don't need a spiritual father." While they argue, they forsake the blessing that a spiritual father brings. A spiritual father will prevent one from experiencing a tremendous amount of pain and heartache. I was kept from trouble because I had a father who took interest in my life. He narrowed me in the ways of the Lord. There were certain restrictions and regulations that were placed on me that kept me from misfortune. He was always there to teach and guide me in the right way when I didn't know what to do. Did I always like it? No. Today, however, I am thankful to my father for keeping me from those things that were wrong.

A child or even a young man left to his own devices will make bad decisions. They lack wisdom to always make the correct decision. The same is true in the spirit. A person who falls under the "little children" or "young men" classification needs someone to help guide them and fashion them in their decision making. We all need a spiritual father to reach the fullness of our potential.

The moral compass and wisdom that was passed to me by my father, I am now passing to my son. This keeps a spiritual heritage alive and growing. Having a father, both natural and spiritual, will keep you from a lot of heartache and trouble.

Always a Son

In the natural, you are first a son before you are a father. A legitimate father will always have been a son first. Someone who was not first a son cannot be a father. It would simply go against natural order to be a father without first being a son. It is not naturally possible, and neither is it possible to be a spiritual father without first going through the maturation process while being a spiritual son.

I have witnessed some supposed "spiritual fathers" in the church hurt other believers. This problem stems from the fact that they were never faithful sons to a legitimate spiritual father. In actuality, they were never spiritual fathers. They may have referred to themselves in that manner, yet the act of invoking the title of "father" never actually made them one. I can sit in a garage and declare I am a car all day long, but I'll never become a car. You can say you are a father all you want, but unless you've been a legitimate son to a legitimate father you cannot yourself be a father.

Even once you are a father, you are still a son. In the natural I am the father of two children, but I am also still a son. There are some people, from a spiritual perspective, who reach the maturity stage of "father" and afterward disown the one who fathered them. This should not be so. The principle of honor and respect to a spiritual father is perpetual; it has no date of expiration. In the natural, the only time that you cease being a son is when your father passes away. However, even when your father is gone, you still honor and respect everything that was done, taught, and imparted to you by your father. One of the ways you do this is by continuing his heritage.

It should be the same in the spirit. Becoming a spiritual father is not a license for you to dishonor, disrespect, and disown the one who poured their life into yours. Now that I am a natural father, I respect and place MORE honor on my father than when I was still living under his roof. I now have an understanding of everything that he sacrificed for me, what he taught me, and how he laid down his life for me. Let it also be so in the spirit. As we reach greater levels of maturity, let us bestow more honor upon our fathers in the faith. You are always a son, and sons always honor their fathers.

Young Men

The final group, the group that we will be examining the most in this book, is that of "young men." We could also call this group spiritual sons and daughters. John identifies several things about this group. This group is "strong," "the Word of God abides in them," and they "have overcome the wicked one."

The first thing John says is that they are "strong." This word literally refers to one who has the strength of soul to sustain the attacks of satan. Sons have been through some battles. They have proven themselves to be able to fight and sustain attacks. Spiritual sons are battle tested. Little children cannot fight, nor have they proven themselves in that manner. However, young men have both fought and proven themselves. They have shown excellence to withstand the attack of the enemy and have overcome. Their faith has been tested and they have come out victorious. They have some experience under their belt. Although their capability is not to the same degree as fathers, they are not "wet behind the ears."

Secondly, John says, "The Word of God abides in them." The word "abides" means *to remain*. The Word has remained in them. This, once again, speaks to experience—the same experience that we talked about with fathers. Sons have passed an element of the test of time. I have seen on numerous occasions an unbeliever walk down the aisle, say a sinner's prayer, come to church, and serve God for a short time then totally backslide and end up in a worse condition. Sons who are young men are beyond this type of conduct and behavior. They have proven that they are going to ABIDE; they are going to LIVE the Word. It is not some passing fad for them; they are living the lifestyle of Christianity. They live the lifestyle of a true son. They live according to the Word.

Lastly, "they have overcome the wicked one." As the Lord began to release this truth to me, this part of the passage really struck me. God began to speak to me about this particular point. He asked me, "Who is the wicked one?" I, of course, responded, "Satan." God's next question was, "What made him the wicked one?" "Pride", I promptly responded. With that answer it suddenly clicked in my spirit. Sons have overcome pride. They have passed the test of subjecting and subduing prideful lusts and rebellion (we will be talking about this in more detail later).

Understand that to be a TRUE SON, you must have first passed the test of overcoming pride. It is one of the oldest tricks the enemy uses. However, if you want to live with the blessing of a son, you must overcome pride. You must overcome the temptation of the wicked one.

Fathers and Sons in the New Testament

Paul and Timothy are a perfect example of a father and son relationship in the New Testament. Paul calls Timothy his son, and two letters that he writes to his spiritual son are in the Bible. Timothy was not Paul's actual flesh and blood son. Paul was not married and thus had no natural offspring. However, Timothy was a son in this sense: he was a pupil and disciple of Paul. Sons are pupils and disciples to their spiritual fathers. Sons are the continuation of a spiritual legacy, just as natural sons are a continuation of a natural father's legacy.

The idea of discipleship should still be alive today. The idea of reproducing spiritually should still be in action. Some have said, "I just need Jesus." Certainly, you need Jesus; that is not debated. Jesus is the ultimate authority. However, this should never be used as an excuse to isolate you from other believers or spiritual fathers. No person has to make a choice between Jesus and a spiritual father. The correct choice is Jesus AND spiritual fathers. We need them both.

I am thankful that Timothy did not embrace the opinion that all he needed was Jesus. Timothy recognized that as a young man, he needed to connect himself to a spiritual father, Paul. Likewise, today we still need to join ourselves to a pastor, apostle, bishop, elder, overseer, or whatever title you may utilize, who will function as a spiritual father. We need to join ourselves to a FATHER. This is a New Testament model and practice that should be continued within the lives of all believers throughout the world today.

[1]Dr. Tan Tee Khoon, *The Christ Difference: The Mark of Authentic Discipleship* (Xulon Press, 2012), 33.

[2]A. Anne Hill, June O'Neill, "Underclass Behaviors in the United States" (CUNY, Baruch College, 1993), http://fatherhood.about.com/od/fathersrights/a/fatherless_children.htm.

CHAPTER 2
HONOR AND OBEDIENCE

Children, obey your parents in the Lord, for this is right. "Honor your father and mother," which is the first commandment with promise: "that it may be well with you and you may live long on the earth." And you, fathers, do not provoke your children to wrath, but bring them up in the training and admonition of the Lord (Ephesians 6:1-4).

Based upon my observation, the generation coming up in the earth today is one of the most dishonoring, disrespectful, and disobedient generations that has ever walked the face of the earth. One of the things that propels this perpetual dishonor and disobedience is the fact that many do not understand what honor and obedience will bring into their lives. Many have become so self-absorbed and motivated by self-ambition that they believe the ideas of honor and obedience are no longer applicable today. The line of thinking is they have somehow moved beyond the point of obedience and honor. Today, many believe that these are archaic ideas that need no longer to be observed. They believe that they have reached a higher state of consciousness.

You have to look no further than the way that many young people talk to their parents, pastors, teachers, and authorities in their lives to see the problem we have with properly honoring authority. This is not to paint some sort of negative, gloomy, and dark picture. However, before we can find the solution we must first identify the problem. Once again, we need to understand how important it is that we honor and obey. For the church to reclaim what we once had in authority and influence, it must start by reinstating the principles of honor and obedience in a generation that is coming up inside of our own walls.

Who Do We Honor and Obey?

Possibly the most quoted scripture in the Bible by parents to their children is located in Paul's letter to the Ephesians, "Honor your father and mother which is the first commandment with promise: that it may be well with you and you may live long on the earth" (Ephesians 6:2-3). I had this scripture drilled in me as a child, and I could quote it at a very young age. When I was disobedient as a young child my parents would pose the question "Joshua, do you want to live a long time?" Like any intelligent person, my response would be affirmative in nature. My parents would follow by quoting the previous passage of Scripture to me. It was a good motivator, and I made the choice to obey.

Likewise, I have used this Scripture on more than one occasion when talking to my children. While this Scripture is true and should be etched into the minds of children, I often believe that we have only looked at it from one perspective: we have viewed it purely from a natural perspective, and totally missed the spiritual dynamic in operation. Is the command to simply obey and honor natural parents? I don't believe so; I believe it is much deeper than that.

The apostle Paul told his spiritual son to treat an elder as a father (1 Timothy 5:1). The word *elder* is the Greek word *presbyteros*. It is where we derive our English word, "presbyter," a person in spiritual authority in the church. This word is used when referring to church leaders as well as people of an older age. While respect should be given to those who are older, Paul is communicating to Timothy the importance of treating those who have labored in the Word as fathers.

The Greek word used in 1 Timothy 5:1 for "father" is the same word used in Ephesians 6 which is *pater*. It means "generator, male ancestor or one who has infused his own spirit into others." Could it be that Paul, a father, is telling Timothy, a son, that you are to honor spiritual fathers? Absolutely. Fathers infuse or pass their spirit into those who are joined to them as sons. Fathers are deserving of obedience and honor from sons and daughters. That is not my opinion; that is what Paul said. If we believe the Bible, we must believe this to be true. Spiritual fathers are worthy and deserving of honor and obedience.

The Principle of Obedience

King Saul is a fascinating figure in the Bible. If Saul continued in the way that he started, he would have been a magnificent godly King. When we are first introduced to Saul the first thing we observe is his obedience to the voice of a father. His natural father asks him to do something that is seemingly insignificant; he simply tells Saul to go look for a donkey. Nothing more, nothing less. Just go find a donkey that is lost.

Most natural sons and those who call themselves spiritual sons would balk at something that is seemingly so insignificant. It's difficult today to get kids to take out the trash, let alone go fetch a stinky, nasty, dirty donkey. Often, the mindset in sons is, "I am too good for that." Yet, **it is Saul's decision to obey and heed an insignificant task that releases destiny in his life.**

While on this seemingly menial task, Saul meets a man named Samuel, the prophet of God. God has already told Samuel the day before that he will see the future King of Israel in the land of Benjamin. So where does Saul go in order to find the donkey from his father's house? He goes to the land of Benjamin. It is in this moment that God tells Samuel that Saul is the one of whom He has spoken; Saul is the one ordained to be King of Israel. Saul ends up wearing the kingly crown because he was faithful to obey and look for a donkey. Your obedience to authorities that God places in your life, both natural and spiritual, will always position you for breakthrough and destiny.

Think about Abram. God tells him to leave a place that he has known his entire life and go to a place that God will show him. He doesn't have a map or any idea where God is taking him; Abram simply has the command to go. Understand this, on the other side of obedience there is always the release of promise. God declares a promise over Abram's life on the heels of his choice to obey.

God tells Abram that he will make him a great nation, that he will be blessed, he will be a blessing, and everyone in the earth will be blessed because of him (Genesis 12:2-3). Incredible promises from an incredible God. All of these promises were not given unconditionally. The linchpin to the declaration of the promise to Abram was obedience. All of these promises were predicated by obedience. You cannot expect to disobey the voice of the Heavenly Father and spiritual fathers and receive blessings from above. It simply doesn't work that way. There is no blessing without obedience.

I've found that in modern Christianity we seem to think that simply believing is enough to release a blessing, breakthrough, deliverance or whatever it is that we need. While we must believe, belief will always lead to actions of obedience. You cannot say that you have faith (that you believe) without actions that back up your faith. This is the very thing that the apostle James declared in James 2:17, "Faith by itself, if it does not have works, is dead." Belief without obedience is useless. Abram believed what God was saying, but his belief compelled him to action. Believing that which God and spiritual authority has said will always compel you to be obedient.

Continual Obedience

"In your seed all the nations of the earth shall be blessed, because you have obeyed My voice" (Genesis 22:18).

At the same time, we must realize that one simple act of obedience is never the end. Anyone can obey once. A single act of obedience does not guarantee the continued unending blessing. It is continual obedience that will release continual blessing. Think about Abram who is later named Abraham. God gives him a son named Isaac. He is the fulfillment of the promise that God made to Abram in Genesis 12. Then, God asks Abraham to sacrifice the seed of promise, Isaac. Abraham has to put the fulfillment of the prophetic word on the altar; he has to sacrifice the realization of the promise that God made to him. Abraham is obedient to his Heavenly Father. We will see that as a result of his continued obedience, God continues to bless Abraham.

The fascinating picture in this story doesn't stop with Abraham's obedience to take Isaac up the mountain. Most theologians agree that Isaac was a strong young adult at the time that God asked for this sacrifice of Abraham. Isaac was required to carry the wood that would be used for a burnt offering; the amount of wood required could not have been carried by a young child. Isaac was a young man strong enough to carry this burden.

Contrastingly, Abraham is well north of a hundred years old. I believe a twenty year old Isaac could have overcome a one hundred and twenty year old Abraham in a struggle or fight. There had to come a point where Abraham's intention became very clear to Isaac. At that point Isaac had a choice: obey or rebel. He chose obedience.

If he was unwilling to lie down, I'm fairly confident he could overcome Abraham without incident. If nothing else, he could surely outrun his father. However, Isaac did not fight Abraham. Isaac was obedient to his father and made the choice to be bound and to lie down on the altar, knowing what would come next. For years Isaac had watched his father, Abraham, be obedient to Father God. The discipline of obedience had been imparted into him as a result of Abraham's continued obedience that was modeled. This was a picture of ultimate obedience that would later be seen in Jesus in the Garden of Gethsemane when He was obedient to the Father to the point of death.

Not only did Abraham pass the test of obedience, Isaac passed the test as well. Afterward, God begins to once again speak the language of blessing. The Lord tells Abraham that He will bless him, his descendants will be numerous as the stars in the sky and sand on the shore, and that all nations will be blessed. God concludes by declaring to Abraham that all these things are enacted "because you have obeyed Me" (Genesis 22:18). All the blessing and all of the increase is due to obedience.

Some have minimized the importance of obedience. This has been done in the name of grace liberating us from any law or requirement. However, Abraham predates the giving of the Law of Moses. He examples a spiritual principle that is required for all generations and dispensations: continual obedience is required to release the perpetual blessing of the Lord.

Obedience will always lead to more blessing. Every time Abraham obeyed, God released more blessing in his life. When you are faced with the decision to obey or disobey, always choose obedience. The more opportunities you have to obey fathers, the more blessing is going to be released in your life. Rejoice in the opportunity given to obey! If you don't believe it, test and see that it is true. I know it's true. Better yet, Abraham and Isaac knew it was true!

The Spirit of YES

Everything that I am doing today in ministry was unlocked on the other side of a "YES" that I gave to authority in my life. Destiny is always unlocked on the other side of obedience. Every time I have said "YES," it has caused a door of opportunity and blessing to come into my life. When I was in the eighth grade, my father and mother asked me if I would be willing to learn to play the bass guitar. In our church body, we had a drummer and my father played the keyboard, but we needed a bassist to complete the rhythm section. I said, "YES." Was this because playing the bass guitar was something I was desirous of doing? No. The idea had honestly never crossed my mind. Now, over fifteen years later, I have never regretted that decision a single day. Playing bass led me to worship leading and song writing. Saying "YES" unlocked a piece of destiny that I had never previously considered.

In late 2001, my father began to discuss television ministry with me. Our church did not have a television broadcast, and no one at the church knew anything about producing a television program. My father asked me if I would be willing to learn. Would you like to guess what I said? "YES!" What else would I say? There is no other appropriate response. I learned how to properly film, edit, and compose a television broadcast. I spent years sitting in an editing room, hearing the Word over and over and over again. I firmly believe those days sitting in an editing room hearing sermons preached repeatedly week after week is that which prepared me for what I am doing in ministry today. Today our television broadcast has touched the lives of many and is seen around the world. Being obedient won't just bless you; it will bless others as well.

Every time a person who has spiritual authority in my life asks me to do something, I look forward to saying "YES." Why? It's because I know on the other side of my obedience, my "YES", there are going to be new doors of opportunity and blessing that open up for me.

Let me encourage you to be a person who lives their life under the principle of "YES." Don't look for a way out of responsibility; respond in an affirmative manner and you'll be amazed at what the "YES" will open up for your life. God will open doors that no man can open or shut on the other side of your "YES."

The Consequences of Disobedience

So Samuel said: "Has the LORD as great delight in burnt offerings and sacrifices, As in obeying the voice of the LORD? Behold, to obey is better than sacrifice, and to heed than the fat of rams. For rebellion is as the sin of witchcraft, and stubbornness is as iniquity and idolatry. Because you have rejected the word of the LORD, He also has rejected you from being king" (1 Samuel 15:22-23).

I want to look back at the life of King Saul and how his choices relating to obedience changed his life. After becoming king of Israel, Saul once again encountered Samuel. This time Samuel, speaking as God's mouthpiece in the earth, gives Saul a very specific directive. Saul is told that God is going to use him and Israel to punish the Amalekites for their mistreatment of the Hebrews as they came out of Egypt. The Amalekites were wicked people. God, through Samuel, commanded Saul to destroy everyone and everything in Amalek. However, he does not follow through with that which God commanded him to do. He only destroyed the "despised and weak," but spares everything else. This proved to be a costly mistake.

God is so grieved at this disobedience by Saul that He says He regrets ever making Saul king. To cause God to regret something He sanctioned is quite severe. To make matters worse, Saul lied about the incident and professed to Samuel that he was obedient (a picture of self-justification). Saul takes it a step further when confronted by Samuel and blames the people (blame-shifts). Saul accepted no responsibility for his disobedience. As a result of his disobedience and failure to take responsibility, God rejects Saul as King of Israel. This seemingly simple act of disobedience caused Saul to lose his kingly anointing and ultimately the throne of Israel (1 Samuel 15:26-28). It would have been much easier to simply obey.

This is such a tragic story. One act of disobedience undoes what an act of obedience had accomplished that positioned Saul to be made King. Think about it! Everything Saul had gained through an act of obedience to his father was lost through one act of disobedience to the word of Father God given through spiritual authority. He veered off the road of obedience that he started his journey on and went down the path of disobedience.

If you consider this from a modern, natural perspective most people would not consider Saul's sin egregious. This reveals that many don't understand God's perspective on obedience. We must have God's view, rather than man's view. Obedience is so important to God that failure to obey can result in great consequences.

Samuel actually tells Saul that God would rather him obey than offer a sacrifice. Obedience in one area of our lives will never substitute for disobedience in another area. There are many believers who occasionally offer sacrifices in praise, worship, giving, prayer, and other biblical acts. However, they are disobedient in many areas of Christian living while thinking they are satisfying the requirements for obedience. God wants our obedience to His voice and the voices of authority that He has established in the earth.

The Voice of God in the Earth

One of the most fascinating things about this account with King Saul is that the command he disobeys was not heard directly from the Lord. He heard the command from the prophet Samuel, a spiritual authority in the land of Israel, who could be considered a spiritual father. So often the contemporary attitude is, "If God didn't tell me to do it then I'm not going to do it. I can hear from God for myself." This mindset and disposition are wrong and erroneous.

Yes, I believe that we all possess the ability to hear the voice of the Lord. However, God speaks things to us through spiritual fathers that He places in our lives. We see this principle exampled here with Samuel and King Saul. God gave Samuel instructions to give to Saul. Why did God do this? He did this to test obedience in the life of the one who was being instructed. Obedience is always the best philosophy.

Understand that anything God speaks to you will meet two criteria. The first thing is that which God speaks to you will be congruent with what He has already stated in the Bible. Secondly, it will bear witness with spiritual authority that God has placed in your life. Of course, you would never obey "authority" that is telling you to do something contrary to what is already clearly stated in the Bible. God will never speak something that is contrary to His written Word.

"Fathers" that give counsel contrary to the Word are not legitimate fathers. The counsel of legitimate fathers will always be in agreement with the written Word of God. If anyone tells you to do something immoral, unbiblical, and/or that violates your conscience, you have reason to question the very presence of that person's voice in your life. However, we must allow the voices of proven legitimate spiritual fathers to speak into our lives.

Don't Make It Difficult

Obey those who rule over you, and be submissive, for they watch out for your souls, as those who must give account. Let them do so with joy and not with grief, for that would be unprofitable for you (Hebrews 13:1).

The writer of Hebrews gives an admonition to simply obey. He says that you are to make it easy on those who are in authority by your obedience. If you don't, it won't be good for you. If you disobey, you make it difficult on yourself. The understanding is that you are not hurting those in authority through defiant and rebellious behavior, you are actually hurting yourself. The "I did it my way" mentality will end in difficulty, heartache, and unfulfilled destiny.

When someone is disobedient they place themselves on the path of the transgressor. Disobedience is sin and transgression against the very order of God. Solomon, the wisest man who ever lived, said, "The way of the transgressor is hard" (Proverbs 13:15). I would advise doing everything possible to stay away from this path. BE OBEDIENT.

Beginning in 1 Samuel 15 and onward, we observe Saul following a trail that constantly spirals downward and eventually reaches the destination of tragic destruction. What brought this about? It was brought about by disobedience to the voice of spiritual authority—the voice of a spiritual father. He placed himself on the "way of the transgressor." That path never ends in a good place. It ends in calamity and heartache. You have a choice: will you live in the destiny and blessing found through obedience or will you experience the destruction found in disobedience?

Obedience is Better than Spiritual Service

I have personally seen repeatedly that one of the ways people excuse their disobedience is through claiming their disobedience was for the purpose of spiritual service. I've observed those who were told to stay inside certain parameters ignore the instruction and disobey. These disobedient sons then blame their disobedience on God. They say things like, "God told me to" or "I just wanted to glorify God." God is glorified more by your obedience than your grand act of service. God is the King of order. Everything God does is in order. We already established that earlier in this chapter. If a person with spiritual authority gives you instruction, you should follow that instruction to the letter. This type of obedience is what glorifies the Lord.

When Saul was disobedient he said it was for the purpose of sacrifice. Saul uses a spiritual excuse for his sin of disobedience. Saul's excuse is spiritual service. I have found that many believers who disobey don't believe that they were disobedient. Instead, they believe they were doing the right thing. They think their service somehow outweighs their disobedience to spiritual authority. Saul thought he had a greater understanding of what would please God; he should have simply obeyed Samuel's instructions. Saul made the grave mistake of thinking that he knew better. He exalted his own opinion over that of the prophet. Saul was wrong. Obedience is always the right answer. Obedience is always pleasing to Father God.

My father always says this, "You will never go wrong by doing what's right." Obedience is always right. Submission to spiritual authority is always right. Even if the authority has an incorrect or outdated method, submission is still right. Why? Because God will honor you for your obedience. God will never honor disobedience and rebellion.

Samuel declared that "rebellion is like the sin of witchcraft" (1 Samuel 15:23). The Bible is very clear about those who practice divination and witchcraft. According to the Law at that time, this sin was punishable by death—execution. You must understand that likewise, rebellion will cause your ministry to die. Acting in rebellion will cause your anointing to be revoked. Just ask Saul. Acting in rebellion is like spraying poison on the tree called your life. When you operate in rebellion you will not bear fruit.

Don't use spiritual service as an excuse for disobedience. God is a God of order, obedience, and honor. God is glorified in one's obedience to spiritual authority. He is not glorified in one's disobedience and rebellion, regardless of how well intentioned or how much one bathes their disobedience and rebellion in religious language.

The Principle of Honor

Much has been made by others as to what exactly defines honor. Entire books have been written on the subject of honor, so I want to look at what honor is at its very core. What is the principle of honor?

The word *honor* means to esteem, value and to hold in high regard. If we recall Ephesians 6:2, Paul tells us that we are to honor those who are fathers within our lives. We are to esteem, value, and hold in high regard those who are also in spiritual authority. Too many people live without awarding honor in any manner or form. Those that choose to live in rebellion do not hold in high regard those who speak into their lives. In fact, they often make the fathers and spiritual authorities who are attempting to help them the villains. This is not honor. In actuality, it is the exact opposite. It is dishonor at the highest degree.

I can remember several moments in my own life as a teenager where I did not exhibit honor in the proper manner. My mother or father would give an instruction and instead of recognizing that they were attempting to help me, I perceived it as them trying to hold me down, control me, and rob me of my individuality. When I behaved in that manner I was displaying the attitude of an immature teenager. Praise God that I did not do this often. When I did have this attitude the Lord was quick to correct it, with some help from my parents, of course.

Yet, how many believers have this attitude towards spiritual leadership? When correction of any sort comes, regardless of how loving, gentle, and considerate, they view it as them being held back from everything that God has for them and their "anointing being quenched." My friend, this is not the case. In actuality, those who display this kind of attitude and disposition are not properly honoring leaders that God Himself has placed in their lives. They are not recognizing them as spiritual mothers and fathers that are endeavoring to keep them from heartache. The spiritual fathers within our lives are trying to help us realize the fullness of the potential which God has placed inside of us. They are not trying to cause us harm. No true father would ever hurt his child. They are actually trying to help us.

It is easy to honor someone when they are telling you how great you are, what a blessing you are, and praising your great qualities and traits. However, this is the question that must be addressed: do you still honor them when they bring correction, or you don't agree with a decision, or you don't understand the reason or purpose for a given directive? The test of obedience and honor is not the adherence to a directive given to which you agree. The true test is your response to a directive to which you despise or disagree. God commanded children— sons and daughters—to honor. There was no distinction given as to when to honor, but simply to honor.

As was stated previously, you are ALWAYS a son, thus you should always honor. Honor is to be continual and ongoing which means you are to honor when you feel like it and when you don't. You must honor when you are being praised and honor when you are being corrected. Honor when everything is going right and honor when it seems everything is falling apart. You must hold in high esteem those who are watching out for your soul even when you don't feel like it—even when it isn't easy. Simply live your life from a principle of honor and God promises that you will be blessed abundantly.

Many people live a lifestyle of **pragmatic** honoring instead of living by the **principle** of honor. What do I mean? This line of thinking is pragmatic: "I'll honor them when they honor me" or "I'll honor them if I think what they are saying is beneficial for me." This is wrong. The principle of honor should be that we choose to honor because the Word of God commands it. When you honor you are sowing seeds of honor to be received in your own life.

I have personally experienced this. When I failed to honor my parents I failed to properly position myself to receive honor from them. This was not their fault, but rather mine. In my ministry, when I have not honored those in authority, ministry opportunities have been closed. When I have honored, I have received honor and numerous ministry opportunities. It all goes back to living by the principle of honor. If you want to receive honor, then you need to sow honor. Live your life by the principle of honor.

Bring Honor to the Legacy

In days of old, there was an idea of bringing honor or shame upon your family name, upon your legacy. If you lived right, you brought honor. If you lived incorrectly, wild and sowing to the flesh, you would bring dishonor and shame. I believe this is not some sort of "old-school" idea, but a principle by which to still live our lives. Just because an idea is "old-school" doesn't mean it is wrong, outdated or irrelevant to us.

The apostle Peter rearticulates a statement that God made in the Old Testament, "BE HOLY, FOR I AM HOLY" (1 Peter 1:16). We bring honor to Father God when we live holy. However, it does not merely stop there. We also bring honor to both natural and spiritual parents when we live holy. If I want to bring honor to my Heavenly Father, I must understand that the way I act reflects on Him. Therefore, I must make wise decisions because my life is not my own (1 Corinthians 6:19-20).

Paul encouraged the church at Corinth to glorify God in their bodies. Why? It is because it brings honor to the Father when we live holy. Likewise, there is honor that is brought to spiritual authority in our lives when we live holy. If you live holy, you won't end up on the ten o'clock news bringing shame upon your family, pastors, church, and the kingdom of God.

Some have said that a message of holiness is bondage. Nothing could be further from the truth. If holiness is bondage, then God is a god of bondage. God said that He was holy, and we should be also. Is God a god of bondage? Certainly not. Our Heavenly Father is the God of freedom and liberty. It's as simple as that. He has no bondage to give to anyone. There is freedom in a lifestyle of holiness that is expressed from a heart of love for the Father.

The bondage of what we have called "legalism" says I must earn love and acceptance from Father God through certain behavior. Holiness says that because He loves and accepts me, I will choose to do that which is pleasing in His sight. We know that His yoke is easy and His burden is light. Living holy is not bondage since He is the one who commands us to be holy.

Understand that LOVE will always compel you to honor. Those who truly understand the agape love of God will live right. Why? Because they love Him. I don't live right because I am merely required to do so; I live right because first of all I am empowered to do so by grace. Secondly, I want to bring honor to God and to those in authority over me. Why? It is because I love and esteem them highly.

Make the Choice

We must make a choice to obey and honor those whom God has placed in our lives as spiritual headship and authority. Make a decision today to conduct your life with the principle of honor and obedience to godly authorities. The choice is entirely up to you. I know that I have lived my life from a place of obedience and honor and God has blessed me, my family, and my ministry as a result. If you will live your life from the same position, I know He will do the same for you because God is no respecter of persons. His principles and precepts work. Obedience and honor will work for you and result in the release of blessing and open doors.

CHAPTER 3
THE MANTLE: A CALL TO SONSHIP

So he departed from there, and found Elisha the son of Shaphat, who was plowing with twelve yoke of oxen before him, and he was with the twelfth. Then Elijah passed by him and threw his mantle on him. And he left the oxen and ran after Elijah, and said, "Please let me kiss my father and my mother, and then I will follow you." And he said to him, "Go back again, for what have I done to you?" So Elisha turned back from him, and took a yoke of oxen and slaughtered them and boiled their flesh, using the oxen's equipment, and gave it to the people, and they ate. Then he arose and followed Elijah, and became his servant (1 Kings 19:19-21).

In this account, Elisha is called to a place of spiritual sonship by a spiritual father, Elijah. Elisha is simply minding his own business farming and tilling the ground in the way his family has most probably done their entire lives. Suddenly, Elijah appears and while walking by he throws his mantle upon Elisha. This is a turning point in the life of Elisha. This completely changes the life of Elisha and sets him on his road of ultimate destiny. It all begins with a mantle.

The Mantle

What was the mantle? It was an outer garment, but it wasn't simply an article of clothing; it was a sign of the anointing and calling of God. The Hebrew word for "mantle" is *addereth*. It means "glory, splendor and magnificence." It was the garment of the prophet and was very special and particular. Elijah's mantle carried a specific anointing. It held a specific calling and is probably one of the most famous pieces of clothing in the entire Word of God.

Jewish tradition believes that the mantle of Elijah, which is later passed to Elisha, was placed inside of a small chamber in the golden altar. Hundreds of years later, Zacharias the father of John the Baptist retrieved this mantle and it was worn by his son during his ministry. This may explain why some Jews believed that John the Baptist was Elijah. It is also a possible explanation to what Jesus said in Matthew 17:12-13, when He declared that Elijah had come already. The Bible tells us that His disciples knew He was talking about John the Baptist. Is it possible Elijah had already come because John the Baptist was operating under the mantle of Elijah? He was literally wearing his mantle. John the Baptist walked in the same authority, power, and anointing wherein Elijah walked.

This mantle was not just some coat, some cape, or some random article of clothing; it was significant. Whenever Elijah cast his mantle on Elisha it is not merely the placing of a coat or cape upon him, it is Elijah prophetically declaring to Elisha, "One day you will wear this." He was declaring, "One day the gifting that I walk in will be your gifting. One day the anointing that I have will be your anointing. One day the same mantle that I wear will be your mantle. One day the miracles that I operate in, you will operate in. You will continue the spiritual legacy that I am currently carrying." I believe that the moment Elijah's mantle touched Elisha he had a glimpse, a prophetic vision, of what God wanted to do in and through him.

I've had mantle moments in my own life. It was during these times when a call of God came forth. These were moments where God revealed to me a picture of what he desired me to do. There was a snapshot of God's plans and purposes for my life that began to be unveiled in these moments. I don't operate in the fullness of the things that were revealed to me at that time; however, God has shown me what is possible if I will be an obedient son. God has revealed what He will accomplish through me as long as I'm faithful.

Elisha's "mantle moment" was not his commissioning into ministry—that comes at a much later date. The mantle being cast was not his cue to go ahead and print business cards, start a website, get on social media and begin to book speaking dates. The mantle was his invitation to a place of sonship; it was an invitation to serve and minister to his spiritual father, the prophet Elijah. Elisha had this moment—this invitation— and he responded with a resounding, "YES."

Sons Follow Fathers

There is significance in the fact that once Elijah cast his mantle; he just keeps on going. Elijah knows what he is supposed to do. He understands his call, and he's not slowing down for anyone. Fathers don't try to coax sons into following. They simply throw a mantle and sons respond. Jesus did this.

And as He walked by the Sea of Galilee, He saw Simon and Andrew his brother casting a net into the sea; for they were fishermen. Then Jesus said to them, "Follow Me, and I will make you become fishers of men." They immediately left their nets and followed Him. When He had gone a little farther from there, He saw James the son of Zebedee, and John his brother, who also were in the boat mending their nets. And immediately He called them, and they left their father Zebedee in the boat with the hired servants, and went after Him (Mark 1:16-20).

We see in this passage of Scripture that Jesus appears to fishermen in the middle of their everyday lives just like Elijah did to Elisha. In the midst of this, Jesus casts a mantle. What is the mantle? "I will make you become fishers of men." Jesus doesn't slow down, He doesn't bargain, nor does He plead. Jesus gives an opportunity for their lives to be eternally changed. In this moment, Simon and Andrew get a glimpse of their destiny and purpose. Then James and John see the same thing. They see what can happen if they choose to be faithful sons. They realize that if they follow they will see the world changed forever. He makes the call, and they follow as disciples—as ones Jesus is pouring into as sons.

Fathers lead the way and sons follow. Fathers don't beg sons to follow; fathers simply lead and sons heed the call to follow. Sons respond appropriately to the call because they want to serve, and they understand destiny is found on the other side of serving.

No Going Back

I believe once you answer the call to sonship, there should be no going back. It is a lifetime commitment, and Elisha understood this. Elisha's family were farmers in an agricultural society. This job was an average job that average people did; it was a normal and respectable occupation. Elisha's family had been farming for years. If you were part of his family, you were a farmer. It is likely that his daddy was a farmer, his grandpa was a farmer and his great-grandfather was a farmer. It was simply what the family did. It was all Elisha ever knew; it was his identity.

When fathers cast a mantle it will always challenge you to go outside of your comfort zone—to go where you've never gone before. There are numerous occasions where God has called me to do something outside of my comfort zone. I am a relatively introverted person. I am not the life of the party. I don't have a need for attention from others, yet God called me to preach and teach the Word. This is way outside of my comfort zone. I have never enjoyed writing, yet God impressed upon me to write a book. This is outside of my comfort zone.

Come and follow the prophet and leave behind your farm tools. This is what Elisha heard which was outside of his comfort zone. All he had ever known was farming. His call to sonship was literally challenging him to leave behind everything that he had ever known—everything he had ever been comfortable doing. Understand that this is a real challenge of Elisha's faith.

Father God is constantly beckoning us to come outside of our comfort zone. You better believe that spiritual fathers will call us outside the comfort zone. Why? It is because spiritual fathers have the heart of Father God. They know Him in His fullness. Thus, they operate in a similar manner.

When the mantle is cast Elisha does something fascinating. Elisha destroys the tools that he had used for years to fulfill the job he thought he was supposed to do. He kills the oxen, destroys his plow, and uses the wood from the plow to create a fire. From this fire he boils the oxen and feeds the people. He makes it impossible to go back to his old ways. He burns his bridges.

Many people today say they are going to follow, yet they leave something to which they can return. If someone leaves something to which they can return, then they will go back to it. The very fact that someone retains the option of returning to something they were called to leave behind reveals that they are not secure in their calling. Elisha was so secure in the calling from God and Elijah that he leaves no plan B.

When Jesus calls Simon and Andrew they dispense with their boat and their business with servants. They burn their bridges; they leave no plan B. James and John are "all in." Their call and future is greater than their present. The mantle is greater than the fishing boat.

Joined to a Vision

Spiritual sons have to join themselves to a vision. They must embrace the vision of the spiritual father that is imparted into their lives. In today's world, the viewpoint is: "What can you do for me?" This should not be the heartbeat of a son. The point of view from a son should be, "How can I minister to the father?" Though the son receives something for serving, his heart is not to receive, his heart is to minister. It has no selfish ambition. The heart is simply to serve the prophet of the Lord.

Elisha has to let his current vision die in order to receive a greater vision for his life. The vision of Elisha was to be a farmer. God had something much more glorious in mind. The heart of a servant releases God's vision which is greater than any selfish ambition.

Elisha has to let his personal vision die. He has to let selfish ambition die. His vision died with the cattle. Think about it: if he had held on to his personal vision, he would have been plowing that field for his entire life. However, the result of letting his vision die promoted him to healing the sick and raising the dead. If Elisha had been hard headed, stubborn, and selfish, he would never have seen the glorious things that he witnessed and experienced. Embracing the life of a true son will always release a greater destiny than can ever be imagined.

I believe there is a generation in the Church today that is not experiencing the fullness of what God has for them because they have failed to link themselves to the vision of a spiritual father. This generation spends their entire life laboring in the field when God has actually called them to raise the dead. I know this thought is not prominent in the Church today, but if we believe the words of Jesus then we must embrace this idea.

Luke 16:12 says, "And if you have not been faithful in what is another man's, who will give you what is your own?" Wow! This type of servant-hood thinking is foreign in the church today. We could say it this way: if you have failed to be faithful to serve another man's vision, God cannot give you your own. It amazes me how every rebellious person in the church has a "vision." They don't have vision, they have ambition. Ambition and vision are two completely different things.

Ambition

Ambition is defined as "an ardent desire for rank, fame, or power." Ambition is a fleshly motivated desire for success. Many believers who say they have vision actually have ambition. At the end of the day, ambition is what drives them. It is not the success of the kingdom of God, nor is it serving spiritual fathers. It is the advancement of their agenda, their message, their ministry, their name, and what "God has given them." This isn't vision; this is fleshly ambition.

It is easy to find yourself driven by ambition, but it is difficult to accomplish your ambition. In order to accomplish ambition, you have to do all the work. Being motivated by ambition will drive you to carry a burden that you were never meant to carry and will make life difficult. Being motivated by ambition will ultimately cause your collapse.

We need not look any further than Balaam to see the trap of fleshly ambition. There is no argument that Balaam was a false prophet. However, what made him a false prophet? Does Balaam hear from God? Yes. The Bible tells us, "God put a word in Balaam's mouth" (Numbers 23:5). Who put a word in Balaam's mouth? The Lord does. God speaks to Balaam and causes him to declare what He was saying. Today, we would call Balaam a true prophet based on that alone. Balaam even calls the Lord his God in Numbers 22. So, Balaam hears from God and declares that He is God. However, it isn't the ability to hear from God, the content of the prophetic word, or his confession towards the Lordship of Jehovah God that makes Balaam a false prophet.

Balaam is a false prophet because of his motivation. He saw money and the favor of King Balak as his opportunity to increase his profile in the earth, and he is driven by ambition. Balaam gives Balak advice that causes the Israelites to commit sin, and the anger of the Lord is aroused against Israel. This was all because of the motivation of Balaam. Peter writes that Balaam "loved the wages of unrighteousness" (2 Peter 2:15). He was motivated by money and power, not the vision of the Lord.

Sons need to be cautious that they are not motivated by selfish promotion or fleshly gain. Be careful as a son that you link yourself with a spiritual father who is motivated by heavenly vision and not earthly ambition. Ambition will cause you to be driven by the promotion of yourself to the point of doing anything to get ahead. If you are motivated by fleshly ambition, you will wind up in the same boat as Balaam, and that is not good company to keep.

Vision

Vision is defined as "a supernatural appearance that conveys a revelation." Vision only comes from God. When you possess a true vision it is not about you, it's all about God and His Kingdom. When you have this attitude, it will make the work of ministry easy. Why? It's because it is God ordered. When you live from a place of vision the lifestyle of a serving son is easy. You realize that godly vision is not self-centered and personally focused, but rather serving for a Kingdom purpose.

For years I have heard my father give this analogy. He said this: "If I go to a restaurant and order something, at the end of the meal I get a check and have to pay for what I ordered. If I can't afford it, then I won't order it. God will always pay for what He orders." When you live pursuing the vision of God for your life He will "pay the check." He will make sure that His will is accomplished if you live to serve His vision. When there is a vision from God doors will open up and He will make a way for that which He ordered. Keep it all about Him and everything that He spoke to you will come to fruition.

The Heart of a Servant

In our modern culture, we believe it is the responsibility of leaders to serve us. While it is true that leaders serve, it is just as much our responsibility to serve leaders and spiritual fathers. It's a two-way street. In reality, leaders equip us for service. Ephesians 4:11-12 says, "And He Himself gave some to be apostles, some prophets, some evangelists, and some pastors and teachers, for the equipping of the saints for the work of ministry, for the edifying of the body of Christ." Their equipping ministry is their service.

The Bible declares that Elisha became Elijah's servant. The King James Bible says that Elisha "ministered unto" Elijah (1 Kings 19:21). The Hebrew word here for "ministered" is *sharath*. It literally means that he served Elijah. Ask yourself this question. Have I served anyone lately?

It amazes me how many sons want to be served whenever one of the primary responsibilities of spiritual sons is to minister to spiritual fathers. How do we serve? Simply find something to do! We make the life of our spiritual authorities easier, not more difficult. This could be any number of different things. Ask and find out what you can do.

While setting up for my daughter's first birthday party, I was moving chairs to the backyard where the party was to be held. My son, Josiah, who was three years old at the time, observed me moving chairs and came to me and said, "Daddy, I want to help." Josiah proceeded to take a chair from me and began to drag it across the yard. It really ministered to me. It made me joyful and it was also helpful. That is the heart of a true son. He observed me doing something and wanted to firstly, imitate me, and secondly, make my job easier.

I know this may seem petty to some, however, I really saw something through it. My son was not able to carry the fullness of the load that I had to carry, but he was willing to carry something. Josiah was able to lighten my load. He, at three years old, was willing to take that chair and do what he could do. He was willing to help me in whatever manner he could. It almost brought me to tears and convicted me at the same time.

How many times have we, as sons, tried to see how little we can do? How often have we attempted to carry as little responsibility as possible and still expect our voices to be heard? If you want your voice to be heard or you want an anointing, you have to be willing to serve. You must be willing to work. "Work" is not some sort of profane word. I have a good friend who I heard say once when he was preaching, "To carry weight, you have to carry weight." That always stuck with me. In other words, if you want to be relevant, if you want to have an anointing, if you want to have a voice, you have to be willing to serve and shoulder the load.

If you aren't willing to "carry weight" you will never be able to "carry weight." There will not be weightiness to your ministry and that which you do if you are not willing to shoulder some of the load. You may not be able to carry the entire load. You may feel like you are only able to carry a single chair, but understand that every chair makes a difference. We must have the heart of a servant. That is the true heart of a spiritual son.

The Water Boy

Throughout the account of Elijah and Elisha, details are a bit scarce on how Elisha serves and ministers to Elijah. Exactly what does Elisha do all of those years? We aren't totally sure. However, we do get one glimpse into what he does in all of his years serving the man of God, Elijah. 2 Kings 3:11 records, "Elisha the son of Shaphat is here, who poured water on the hands of Elijah."

Elisha finds something to do. He begins to bear weight. The only thing we know about Elisha during his time of serving and ministering to Elijah is that he poured water on the hands of the man of God. It may have seemed small and insignificant. It is probably something that no one else wanted to do. He is essentially the water boy of Elijah. However, Elisha is willing to do what his hand finds to do.

It doesn't matter how insignificant the task may seem, you find something to do, somewhere to serve, and you do it with EVERYTHING inside of you. God will bless you as you are faithful to serve. Elisha is faithful to pour water on the hands of Elijah. There is nothing glorious about this job. There is nothing of high esteem associated with being the water boy. But, it is something that was necessary. This simple act of service is a blessing to the life of Elijah.

At one time, Elisha had helped a multitude as a farmer. In his new role, he is simply a water boy. In the natural it appears that he has taken a demotion. However, Elisha understands that his new role is not insignificant. He understands that it is preparation. This is preparing him for the destiny that God has for him. The entire time he is serving, he is also observing. He is watching as Elijah lays hands on the sick. He observes closely as the ministry of the prophet is demonstrated through Elijah. He gets a front row seat to watch Elijah operate under the mantle that he will one day have the honor and privilege of wearing.

I believe that if, as sons, our perspective will change, we will realize that the feeling of being held down, crushed, and demoted is simply God's process within our lives. God is preparing us for a powerful ministry and anointed life.

Answer the Call

Answering the call to sonship is not an easy decision. The road of sonship is not always an easy road, nor is it necessarily a glamorous road. However, there is no more rewarding road than the road of service as a son. As I have chosen to be a faithful son, God has released incredible levels of blessing in my life. Choose to embrace the mantle, link yourself to a spiritual father, serve, and be a son.

CHAPTER 4
THE SEED LIFE

Another parable He put forth to them, saying:"The kingdom of heaven is like a mustard seed, which a man took and sowed in his field, which indeed is the least of all the seeds; but when it is grown it is greater than the herbs and becomes a tree (Matthew 13:31-32).

Here, Jesus is revealing to us the principle of the power of the seed. Everything eternal, everything of worth in life operates under the principle of the seed. The kingdom of Heaven is likened unto the seed. Therefore, everything in the Kingdom operates under this same principle.

Jesus understands this because it is the very order that Father God established at the time of creation. In Genesis 1, God creates the earth. He does not simply say, "Every time I want something to grow I will speak it into existence." To the contrary, God declares that everything on the earth would spring forth because of seed that is planted. We read in Genesis how God created the Garden of Eden. He does not speak Eden into existence. The Bible tells us, "The Lord God **planted** a garden eastward in Eden" (Genesis 2:8).

At the very beginning of creation, God declares and demonstrates that He would do things by way of seed. Everything that reproduces, buds, and flourishes is going to transpire by the medium of the seed. Both natural and spiritual, the principle of the seed cannot be escaped. It is an irrefutable, inescapable spiritual law.

This is equally true in the New Covenant. Galatians 6:7 declares that God is not mocked and you are going to reap what you sow. Under the New Covenant things are still accomplished by the principle of the seed.

If you think that you can escape the principle of the seed, you are only fooling yourself. Just like you cannot ignore the law of gravity, the law of the seed cannot be ignored. I can say all I want that gravity doesn't exist, yet gravity will still exist. I cannot say that gravity is nonexistent, jump off a building, and be unscathed. I will be injured and possibly die as a result because the law of gravity works regardless of what I believe or say. You cannot declare yourself free from the law of the seed. Whatever you sow, you will reap.

So, what is the principle of the seed? To put it simply, whatever you sow in actions and behavior will produce a harvest in your life. This principle can be your greatest friend, or your worst enemy. It's all according to how you work it. When you are willing to work this principle to your advantage, something great can be produced from that which is least. That which is least, once sown, becomes greatest of all. This is the summation of the parable and principle of the seed.

Everything is Seed Sown

We have often used the principle of the seed when it is expedient for us. We sow seed believing for financial release when we believe for financial breakthrough. While this is true and a good principle to activate in our lives, sowing a financial seed while mismanaging the funds that we presently possess will not produce financial blessing. When anyone sows a seed of mismanagement it cannot produce the harvest of blessing. No amount of giving can undo the seed which was sown. You must learn to manage. If you believe in the principle of the seed, you must realize that you cannot pick and choose when it applies and when it doesn't. EVERY action and lack of action is seed sown.

You don't get to choose when you sow seed. You are always sowing seed. We need to be aware of this fact and live accordingly. Realize this: YOUR LIFE IS SEED. Having a revelation of this will change the way that you live. If we really believe that every action we perform will cause a harvest to come forth, we will live differently. We would live on purpose and live intentionally if we really believed it. We need to possess the understanding that we will reap a harvest for every action that we sow.

A seed produces after its own kind. If you want apples, you don't sow orange seeds, you sow apple seeds. Why? Apple seeds will produce an apple tree. It produces after the nature of the seed. If you want honor, sow seeds of honor. If you want blessing, sow seeds of blessing. It is a very simple and elementary principle, but one that will change your life if you live by it.

You are seed. You may seem small and insignificant just like the mustard seed, the smallest seed. Yet, just like the mustard seed, if you allow yourself to be planted you will become a great tree. In order for the best results to come into your life you must be PLANTED. However, for a seed to be planted, it must be put under dirt.

Under Dirt

Seed is fascinating. It is actually unproductive and useless unless it is planted even though it has tons of potential inside of it. However, all the potential inside of the seed will remain inside of the seed until it is activated. An inactivated seed is unprofitable and has no practical value. In order to activate the potential inside a seed, it must go to one place: under dirt. If a seed is not put under dirt, the fullness of the potential inside of the seed will never be realized.

There are many believers who refuse to be put under dirt. Consequently, they remain an unplanted seed. They are so interested in "being seen" and exercising "their ministry" that they remain a seed. They never go under dirt. They have greatness inside, but the fullness of purpose and destiny inside of them is never unlocked because they refuse to go under dirt. Instead of seeing God move in the fullness of what He has placed inside of them, they die with all of that potential still locked inside.

Inside of the mustard seed is the potential for a great, magnificent, fruit producing, seed-bearing mustard tree. However, to produce fruit and more seed, it must first go under dirt to develop. Inside of your life is the potential for incredible works that will change the world. Everyone has that potential.

Whether the seed reaches potential is not determined by your gender, race, socio-economic standing or any other natural thing. The factor that decides whether seed reaches potential is simple: was it put under dirt?

What do I mean "under dirt?" Has the seed of your life undergone a process of being in a place that is dark that no one sees in order to form a root system from which you can bloom? When a seed germinates (which happens under the soil), the first thing that emerges from the seed is the embryonic root. This is also called the radical or primary root. Why does this form first? It is because the root draws nourishment from the soil where it is planted. This is important because as it draws water and nutrients from the soil, it releases the cotyledons or seed leaves. This is the part of the plant that everyone sees. However, what everyone sees above the soil is impossible without that which you can't see beneath the dirt. Who created this growth system? God did! Do you think he was trying to teach us something about our own lives by designing the process in which seed, that no one sees, becomes a great tree that everyone sees? Absolutely!

Your public ministry and public service will be powerless without roots from which to draw. This process can only happen by going under dirt and allowing for a process of development. It doesn't happen overnight. It can sometimes be a long process. However, if you attempt to circumvent the process, you will not flourish to the fullness that God desires.

We must be willing to undergo a process of maturation that others don't see. Through this process, roots that draw nourishment are formed so that the ministry that will be seen by others can live. Far too many people want the leaves without the process; they want fruit without roots. It doesn't work that way. It is out of order, both scientific natural order and spiritual order. Let me give you an example from my own life.

Today I preach a sermon and people only see the forty-five minutes that I spend delivering the sermon itself. People are blessed and ministered to during these forty-five minutes. What people fail to see are the hours of study that I have spent on that particular message, the time in prayer, or the years that I have spent as a student of the Word. Neither do they see the years of experiences that birthed that message. The time spent in study and prayer was the seed part of my life under dirt. The actual delivery of the sermon was the tree. The people whose lives are impacted by the message are the fruit.

Without the study and the dedication to be a student of the Word, I wouldn't have been able to deliver the sermon. I may have been able to stand up and talk, but it wouldn't have produced any fruit. The reason that any sermon I've ever ministered has had any fruit is the root system that was feeding it. The roots created a way for fruit to come forth.

Let's look at Elisha's life as seed. Elisha spends years as the water boy for Elisha. He simply pours water on the hands of Elijah. This is the picture of a life under dirt. There is nothing glorious about it. There is nothing that is inherently magnificent about it. He is simply a servant that probably few even notice, even less know his name. All the while he is observing everything done by Elijah. He is hearing every prophetic word that Elijah releases in the earth. He is there when Elijah performs miracles. No one notices him. However, he is there the entire time observing Elijah.

Elisha serves and lives a life under dirt. He goes on to be a powerful prophet and minister in his own right. This is fed by a root system that was formed under dirt. The root system was cultivated by years under dirt. Likewise, you can't have a powerful, productive, destiny-filled life without a strong root system. You have to go under dirt. In order to be productive in the kingdom of God, you must first be planted under dirt. Nothing flourishes without first being under dirt.

Jesus: Under Dirt

Before Jesus ever preaches a sermon, performs a miracle or calls a disciple to follow Him, He first goes under dirt. First of all, Jesus spends thirty years under dirt in preparation for three years of ministry. We have it backwards. We want to spend six months in preparation for sixty years of ministry. I don't believe these thirty years were merely Jesus biding time until His ministry time arrived. These were years of formation. Jesus goes through the process of developing a root system upon which His ministry could be launched.

The very first time we ever see Jesus minister is found in Luke chapter two when as a young boy, He begins to minister at the temple. When His parents, Mary and Joseph, find Him, they take Him home. Jesus doesn't question or rebuke them; He complies. Jesus goes back under dirt. He is completely subject to His parents. Joseph is not even His actual parent, but rather a father figure that His Heavenly Father placed in His life. Joseph acted much like a spiritual father or we could say a steward in the life of Jesus. As a result of being willing to go through this process, the Bible tells us that Jesus "increased in wisdom and stature, and in favor with God and men" (Luke 2:52). This is all the result of His willingness to go back under dirt and continue to develop.

Jesus is able to impress the scholars, but He wasn't ready for His ministry to be manifested. The tree of Jesus' ministry is not yet ready to bear fruit. Understand that just because you can impress some people with your wisdom, gifting, or ability does not mean you have arrived. Neither does it mean that your season of developing roots is over. When those that God has placed in your life pull you back, be willing to continue to live in the place of the seed. If you do, the result will be even more glorious when the time for blossoming comes.

In Matthew 4, we see Jesus led into the wilderness by the Holy Spirit. This is the time where seed has developed its root system and is preparing to break through the surface. Everything the root system is supposed to do is put to the test. Jesus is tempted and tested and then figuratively breaks through the soil. It is fascinating that immediately after this Jesus goes to Galilee and preaches His first message. He has been seed under dirt and now the leaves begin to show in a great, powerful, and glorious manner.

If Jesus, the Son of God, is the perfect example of a son and He went under dirt, how much more should we be willing to go under dirt? There is no such thing as a "quick path" in the Kingdom. Everything undergoes the process of the seed. If Jesus lived this process, there is no way for us to circumvent or escape it.

Embrace the process of the seed. Be a person of seed. Find joy in the process. I don't believe Jesus was surly and grumpy during the years of the process. Neither should we be sour during this period. I believe Jesus had joy in the process. Count the process as joy and appreciate it.

Short-cutting the Process

In the natural, seed cannot uproot itself because it is tired of not being seen. Unfortunately, we, as people, can uproot the seed of our life. There are many people who have done just that. It is not worth taking yourself out of soil. I have known great young men and women of God with great calls on their lives who are not doing anything today for the Kingdom because they uprooted themselves. Today, people with less natural ability and talent are doing more for God because they endured the process of the seed. I don't want this to be said of me or you. Stay with the process.

Many of these who uproot themselves have developed a strong root system and were on the verge of their leaves—their ministry—springing into visibility. If they just stay where they are planted, they would see the budding and blossoming in their life. It is not the biggest seed that bears fruit. It is the one that stays planted. It is the one that endures the process. STAY PLANTED!

Overcoming Offense

Luke 7:23 says, "Blessed is he who is not offended because of Me." No believer would ever admit to being offended by the Lord. However, when we allow ourselves to be offended by a process that He ordained and He created, at the base of it we are offended at Him. You cannot say that you are offended by a law without saying that you are offended at the writer of the law. Let's take this a step further. If you get offended at the dirt (the leaders) that God has called you to be under, you are getting offended with the Lord Himself. You are offended at the very method and manner that He has chosen to implement the process. Thus, you are offended at Him. I recognize that this is strong, but it is the truth.

In my house we have rules. If my kids get mad about the rules, they are actually getting mad at me for making the rules, not the rule in and of itself. Any other conclusion we arrive at is just fooling ourselves. When we allow ourselves to become offended with people God has called us to be under, we are really getting offended with God. We are saying, 'God, You didn't know what You were doing when You put me under the authority of these people. Why did You do this?' It is the apex of human arrogance to think that we know better than Almighty God. However, more people uproot the seed of their life over offense than anything else.

Jesus said those who are "not offended" in Him will be blessed. The inverse is true. If you become offended at Him, His working, and His servants and uproot yourself, you will not be blessed. You will not flourish and you will simply remain a seed. You will be a rebellious Christian who never realizes their full potential. All the potential in the world locked up inside of you, but nothing of use. Lord, let that not be said about any of us.

The Pressing

Once you have allowed yourself to live a life of seed, you will begin to bud and bring forth fruit. I believe the reason you bring forth fruit is in order for the fruit to be processed to produce oil—to produce anointing. An anointing cannot be bought or even prayed into existence. It comes as a result of processing fruit.

In the Bible, when someone was anointed there was always oil that was present. Why? The anointing is always represented by oil. The word translated "anointed" literally means to rub with oil. When David was anointed King, oil was poured on his head. The anointing to do the job was being released in his life which was represented by oil. Oil can only be produced in one way: through the process of pressing. Let's look at this process.

The process of creating olive oil starts with a farmer gathering olives from the olive tree. Olive oil cannot exist without first having the olive fruit. If your life has no manifestation of fruit then there is no basis for oil; no basis for anointing. If you aren't bearing fruit, you must begin to bear fruit in order to have a base to start the process of producing an anointing.

After the farmer gathers the olives from the tree, he cleans the olives making sure that any dirt or impurity is taken away. If there is impurity present, it will taint the oil. Unfortunately, many believers and ministers circumvent and avoid this process. As a result they end up with tainted oil. Yes, they have an anointing. Yes, they preach the word. Yes, they have signs, wonders, and miracles. However, they fall and bring reproach on the Body of Christ. Why? It's because they never allowed a father to get in their dirty spots and clean away the impurity.

It is uncomfortable when someone begins to scrub you to wash away the dirt. It can even be painful at times. However, it is necessary. If you don't allow impurity within your life to be cleansed, you will end up with tainted oil—a tainted anointing. Let the Heavenly Father and spiritual fathers that He has ordained clean the impurities from your life.

Finally, once the fruit has been harvested and cleaned, they undergo the process of crushing. This is where oil is finally produced. Everything inside of that fruit is pressed and put under pressure until it becomes oil. No one likes "the squeeze" placed upon them. No one likes the process of pressing. However, it is worth the result: oil. The pressing produces anointing. Let your flesh decrease so that the anointing can increase.

It takes approximately twenty olives to produce one ounce of olive oil. In your kitchen, you probably have a sixteen ounce bottle of olive oil that you use to cook with. It took approximately three hundred and twenty olives to produce that oil. That's a lot of fruit for that amount of oil. If you want a lot of oil, an extraordinary anointing, you are going to have to undergo a lot of fruit bearing and a lot of crushing and pressing. It's worth the process to have the oil. The anointing is worth it all.

Choose the Seed Life

Make a choice today that you are going to be a person of the seed. You will go through the process of being under dirt. If you do so, it will produce roots that produce fruit that is apparent to everyone. This fruit will be processed, cleansed, and pressed in order to create oil—an anointing. The seed life is worth the reward.

CHAPTER 5
OVERCOMING PRIDE

Will any man of you who has a servant plowing or tending sheep say to him when he has come in from the field, Come at once and take your place at the table? Will he not instead tell him, Get my supper ready and gird yourself and serve me while I eat and drink; then afterward you yourself shall eat and drink? Is he grateful and does he praise the servant because he did what he was ordered to do? Even so on your part, when you have done everything that was assigned and commanded you, say, We are unworthy servants [possessing no merit, for we have not gone beyond our obligation]; we have [merely] done what was our duty to do (Luke 17:7-10, The Amplified Bible).

Jesus is dealing with an attitude of pride in this passage of Scripture. If Jesus took time to deal with pride, then we must take time to remove pride from our lives. Faithful sons must be able to overcome pride. There is simply no room for pride in our hearts. I believe that pride is one of the primary tools the enemy uses to get us off track and keep us from the fullness of what God has prepared.

When we honor, when we are obedient, when we are faithful to be seed, when we are faithful to serve, and when we allow ourselves to be crushed, we are simply fulfilling our responsibility as sons and believers. We require no additional praise. The result of the process is all we need. We're not doing any of these things for personal praise, glory, or honor. We are doing it because Father God commanded it. We are doing it because it is the example that Jesus set before us.

Prideful Seed

I believe that some have allowed themselves to be seed put under dirt, yet they don't bear fruit. Why do they not bear fruit? It is because they are prideful seed. In Matthew 13:24-30, Jesus gives the parable of the wheat and the tares. Jesus paints a picture of a field. In this field, the owner has sown seed. Yet while he is sleeping, his enemy comes in and plants seed in the exact same field. The wheat spring up from seed, and the tares (the seed of the enemy) spring up, as well. The master of the field allows the wheat and tares to grow side by side. Then when harvest time comes—when the time for fruit comes—the wheat is processed and put into barns. Meanwhile, the tares are thrown into the fire because there is nothing good in the tare.

I think it had to be interesting to be a disciple of Jesus. He would talk in these grandiose stories—parables. I can imagine sitting and thinking, 'Wow! That was awesome. What was he talking about?' Thankfully for us, and the disciples, Jesus gives an explanation. Jesus tells His disciples that the sower of good seed is the Son of Man, the field is the world, and the good seed are the sons of the Kingdom. But, the tares are the sons of the wicked one. He also tells us that the enemy who sows them is satan.

It is important that we realize that the appearance of the wheat and the tare is almost identical. The difference is the character of the seed and the fruit that it yields. The wheat and the tare were in the same field. They were planted together, progressed together, and ultimately produced together. One of the differences is that when wheat reaches full maturity, the head of the wheat begins to bend down because the fullness of the fruit it produces is heavy. The tare stands straight up because it produces no fruit and it has no weight. The bending down that wheat does is a perfect picture of humility. True fruit will cause you to be humble. Meanwhile, the tare stands tall and prideful. The reality is the tare has no reason to be prideful; it produces nothing and is good for nothing but to be burned.

The subject of this parable that Jesus articulated was the character of the seed. It has nothing to do with the growth process and everything to do with the character of the seed and the sower. The master of the wheat was the Son of Man, Jesus. Jesus produces a seed that was after His heart: humble and fruit bearing. The master of the tare was the enemy, the devil. This seed produces pride and emptiness. Lucifer is the master of pride and thus produces the fruit of pride in the seed that is of his character.

Lucifer: The Master of Pride

Moreover the word of the LORD came to me,
saying, "Son of man, take up a lamentation for the

king of Tyre, and say to him, 'Thus says the Lord
GOD: "You were the seal of perfection, full of
wisdom and perfect in beauty. You were in Eden,
the garden of God; every precious stone was your
covering: the sardius, topaz, and diamond, beryl,
onyx, and jasper, sapphire, turquoise, and emerald
with gold. The workmanship of your timbrels and
pipes was prepared for you on the day you were
created. "You were the anointed cherub who covers;
I established you; you were on the holy mountain of
God; you walked back and forth in the midst of
fiery stones. You were perfect in your ways from the
day you were created, till iniquity was found in
you. "By the abundance of your trading you became
filled with violence within, and you sinned;
therefore I cast you as a profane thing out of the
mountain of God; and I destroyed you, O covering
cherub, from the midst of the fiery stones. "Your
heart was lifted up because of your beauty; you
corrupted your wisdom for the sake of your splendor;
I cast you to the ground, I laid you before kings,
that they might gaze at you. "You defiled your
sanctuaries by the multitude of your iniquities, by
the iniquity of your trading; therefore I brought fire
from your midst; it devoured you, and I turned you
to ashes upon the earth in the sight of all who saw
you. All who knew you among the peoples are
astonished at you; you have become a horror, and
shall be no more forever""" (Ezekiel 28:11-19).

Ezekiel is prophesying against the King of Tyre. When
you first read this it appears that Ezekiel is making a prophetic

declaration against a man. However, how could another man have been in the Garden of Eden? How could a man be the anointed cherub that covers? Most theologians believe that this is a dual prophecy. In this declaration Ezekiel is comparing the pride of the King of Tyre to the pride of Lucifer. Some have hypothesized that the King of Tyre was actually possessed by satan himself. Nonetheless, we see a picture here of Lucifer or satan, being cast down from heaven.

Why in the world would Lucifer give up what he had? He is a Cherub. Ezekiel even says that he is the "anointed cherub who covers." The word that is translated *covers* means protector. It is possible that Lucifer is the one who guards the presence of God. Many theologians believe that Lucifer is a ceremonial guard in heaven. We also know that Lucifer is beautiful and covered with all sorts of beautiful stones. Ezekiel declares that he is perfect. He possesses a perfect position that should have never been abandoned.

Why is Lucifer perfect? It is because God made him that way. Everything that Lucifer has was because God gave it to him; it wasn't because of anything that he did to earn or gain it. This should have been something that brought humility to him; however, Lucifer becomes puffed up. He fails to realize that everything he possesses comes from Father God. He falls for the age-old trap of believing that it was all about him and what he could do. This pride leads to rebellion, and Lucifer is cast from the presence of God and heaven. This manifestation of pride will ultimately lead to him being eternally cast in the lake of fire to be burned. The entire reason that Lucifer is cast from heaven is because of his prideful heart. A heart full of pride will separate you from God and His presence.

The Manifestation of Pride

When anyone declares that they are not needful of something God has ordained, it is the ultimate manifestation of pride. God ordained the concept of spiritual fathers. God ordained the principle of the seed. God ordained the crushing to produce oil. When someone says that they have no need of any of these things, they are operating in a spirit of pride. If you find yourself walking in this, you should repent and allow God to work in your life the way that He designed. He who is humbled will be exalted. James said that if we humble ourselves then God will lift us up (James 4:10). When you are humble, there is no need to promote yourself; God will do it for you. Simply walk in humility and allow yourself to be elevated by your Heavenly Father.

Jesus: The Picture of Humility

There has never been a son more humble than Jesus. He is the model by which we all should try to base our lives. The very fact that Jesus, the perfect spotless lamb, would come to earth in the likeness of sinful flesh to redeem those who are undeserving reveals His humility. Jesus continues to show humility throughout His life and ministry.

In Matthew 3, Jesus appears in Galilee looking for John to baptize Him. Jesus, the perfect spotless Lamb of God, tells a mere man that He wants to be baptized by him. John the Baptist is astonished by this and tells Jesus, "I need to be baptized by you." I would probably respond in the same manner if I was in John's sandals. John agrees to baptize Jesus and then something incredible happens.

When He was baptized Jesus came up immediately from the water; and behold, the heavens were opened to Him, and He saw the Spirit of God descending like a dove and alighting upon Him. And suddenly a voice came from heaven, saying, "This is My beloved Son, in whom I am well pleased" (Matthew 3:16-17).

John the Baptist is the one who prepared the way for Jesus as he preached the message of repentance. He is the forerunner to the Son. Spiritual fathers are to be forerunners for spiritual sons and daughters. We can look at John the Baptist here as a picture of a spiritual father.

Jesus, the promised seed, the one of whom John the Baptist has been prophesying, asks John to baptize Him. In order to fully realize the significance of Jesus' actions, one must understand the meaning of John's baptism. There was no baptism as we know it today. Our New Testament understanding of water baptism is the signification of dying to sin and coming alive in Christ. However, the baptism of John was not encased with this understanding.

The baptism of John is an act called proselyte baptism. It was part of the process by which those outside of covenant would come into a place of covenant. This is the process whereby a Gentile was grafted into Judaism. Who could have been more in covenant than Jesus? No one! No one had more right standing and covenant with God than Jesus. He is God's own Son; He is actually God incarnate. Yet, Jesus comes to John and humbles Himself to the process. He humbles Himself to the one who has prepared the way—the one who has come before Him.

Jesus humbles Himself to the picture of a spiritual father. John the Baptist is the prophetic voice in the earth at that particular time. John is the one who is anointed by the Holy Spirit. Jesus has not yet been anointed for His earthly ministry. The anointing does not begin to be revealed until after He submits Himself to the ministry of the one who is the prophet of God in the earth, John the Baptist.

Jesus displays an incredible act of humility. Immediately on the other side of this display of humility a voice comes from heaven expressing God's delight in His Son. When we are humble we invoke an open heaven and God expresses His delight in us and our lives of humility. This can only come through a humbling process. God never expresses His blessing and pleasure in a prideful son. Quite the opposite is true.

There are numerous times throughout the ministry of Jesus where He displays an attitude and disposition of humility. Jesus gets in the dirt with the woman caught in adultery. He washes the feet of His disciples. He ultimately endures a painful and humiliating death because it was the will of the Father, not because He deserved it. Jesus was the ultimate picture of a true and humble son.

W.W.J.D.

I can remember when I was younger; there was a very popular fashion trend that began to sweep across the nation. It seemed as if suddenly one day, everyone was wearing bracelets that said W.W.J.D. This, of course, stood for "What Would Jesus Do." Unfortunately there were a lot of people who merely wore the bracelets yet didn't live that lifestyle. This should not have been some sort of empty fashion statement, but rather a mindset from which people lived their lives. Unfortunately for many it was nothing more than a bracelet on their wrist. The answer to the question, "What would Jesus do?" is found in the Bible. Simply examine the life of Jesus and find out.

If we are going to ask, "What would Jesus do?" we must understand that everything that Jesus did was birthed from a place of humility. If you want to be like Jesus, then you need to be humble. Jesus was not full of pride. He was the most humble person to ever walk the face of the earth.

Sons Overcome Pride

We briefly mention in chapter 1 of this book that John writes to young men because "they have overcome the wicked one." One of the distinguishing characteristics of young men, of sons, is that they have overcome satan. What is the thing that made him wicked? Pride! Before pride entered his heart, he was glorious and beautiful in everything. Pride corrupted Lucifer and made him satan. Pride will ultimately corrupt.

In order to overcome the wicked one, you must overcome pride. I have never met someone prideful who was able to consistently overcome the enemy. If you allow pride into your life, you will become like the seed of the tare that was planted by the enemy. When you become the seed of the enemy you get his fruit. We learned earlier that his fruit is of no good, carries no weight, and manifests itself with pride.

You must understand that when a spiritual father begins to speak into your life, the enemy will attempt to use a spirit of pride to get you to shut your ears. If you have ever allowed a spiritual father or mentor speak into your life, you know exactly what I'm talking about.

In my early years of ministry, when spiritual authority would begin to address things in my life, the spirit of pride would want to raise its ugly head. I would begin to think things like "I'm too good for this. Who do they think they are? If they think they can do better, then they can do it themselves. There's a new way of doing things and they are out of touch." These are all prideful thoughts. I imagine these are some of the very thoughts Lucifer thought before he rebelled in Heaven. Thankfully, the Holy Spirit convicted me and I was able to bring my thoughts into subjection and ultimately defeat pride.

If you don't defeat pride, your anointing will be tainted and perverted. If pride reigns in your life, you will share the same fate as the prince of pride, satan. There will be no manifest presence in your life. I know this is not what I want for my life, and I also believe it is not what you want for your life. Get rid of pride and live with a humble and teachable spirit. It's for your making, not your breaking.

Avoid Destruction

Proverbs 16:18 says, "Pride goes before destruction, and a haughty spirit before a fall." Pride will destroy you; it will bring destruction into your life. Pride is sinful. Dr. Bill Hamon, my father's spiritual father and a true father of the faith whom I greatly respect, addressed my father and all of his staff on the heels of many scandals breaking in the Church at large that were bringing reproach on the entire body of Christ. Dr. Hamon made this statement, "Get rid of your sin, or your sin will get rid of you." I have heard my father tell this story many times and it has always stayed with me. If you don't get rid of pride, your pride will get rid of you. It will ultimately cause you to lose your anointing.

Saul must find this out the hard way. As we mentioned in an earlier passage, Saul had the kingdom of Israel ripped from him when he disobeyed the voice of the Prophet Samuel. Saul's disobedience was a manifestation of pride. How did he disobey? He didn't kill ALL of the Amalekites. When you fast-forward years later, it is an Amalekite that kills Saul. Think about it!

In 2 Samuel 1:8-10, we meet an Amalekite who killed Saul. This young Amalekite boy tells David, "I stood over him and killed him!" Wow! This Amalekite who kills Saul should have been dead. Saul should have ordered his execution back when Samuel delivered the Word of the Lord. However, because Saul doesn't deal with his sin, his sin deals with him. Saul is prideful and the fruit of his pride was to not destroy all of the Amalekites. He does not obey the Prophet, the voice of a father, because he thought he knew better. As a result, an Amalekite kills Saul. If you don't deal with pride, pride will deal with you.

Choose Humility

If you choose a lifestyle of pride, you will be put down to shame. However, if you choose a lifestyle of humility, of defeating and putting pride down, God will bless you and exalt you. Choose humility today! Choose to live the life that produces fruit, not the life that produces destruction.

CHAPTER 6
FOLLOW THE TRAIL

I do not write these things to shame you, but as my beloved children I warn you. For though you might have ten thousand instructors in Christ, yet you do not have many fathers; for in Christ Jesus I have begotten you through the gospel. Therefore I urge you, imitate me. For this reason I have sent Timothy to you, who is my beloved and faithful son in the Lord, who will remind you of my ways in Christ, as I teach everywhere in every church (1 Corinthians 4:14-17).

Paul writes to the church at Corinth and gives them the command to imitate him. The problem with this scenario is that Paul is not present at Corinth. So, if Paul is not present at Corinth, then how are the Corinthians supposed to imitate him? How can they follow the example of Paul if he is not there in Corinth? The answer is really quite simple: follow Timothy. Timothy is a spiritual son of Paul and he knows the ways of Paul. He understands Paul, and he operates in the same spirit and mantle of Paul. Thus, the Christians at Corinth are expected to imitate Timothy.

The Sincerest Form of Flattery

Timothy is living a life that imitates Paul as Paul imitates Christ. Timothy, as a spiritual son, is to model the behavior of his spiritual father, Paul. This is how the Corinthians are going to know how to act like Paul. The reason we can act like the Father is because He sent His Son, Jesus, as the ultimate model of sonship.

Sons will imitate their fathers. There is a scene in the movie *Jaws* where after a tough day at work, Chief Brody is sitting at his dinner table drinking from a glass. As Brody takes a drink, his son who is also at the table takes a drink in the same manner. The son imitates the way Brody holds his hands and then covers his face. Brody then begins to move his fingers and the son follows in the same fashion. It's a picture of this: sons imitate fathers.

Sons will always imitate their fathers. This is a biblical concept, not merely some form of coincidence. The writer of Hebrews tells us to "imitate those who through faith and patience inherit the promises" (Hebrews 6:12). If you want to obtain the promise, then you must imitate the lifestyle and commitment of a spiritual father who has come before you. Sons are intended to imitate fathers.

As I consider myself, there are so many of my personal characteristics that I have that are very similar to my father. When I first began to preach, I noticed that the way I stood in the pulpit, the way I walked the platform, and even certain words and sayings I used were almost identical to that of my father. Was this intentional? Certainly not. However, I do believe that it is godly. God designed sons to imitate fathers.

Jesus propagated this principle and idea. Jesus said, "He who has seen Me has seen the Father" (John 14:9). There are obviously deep things in this statement regarding the nature of the Trinity in all of its mystery. However, at its most simplistic root, Jesus is saying, "Since I am the Son, when you see Me, you are seeing the Father." Why? It is because sons are inherently wired to mimic the actions and behaviors of their fathers. They've heard them talk and seen them live. There is a value system that has been imparted by fathers to their sons that must continue. Sons carry the legacy. They are meant to be a continuation of their fathers.

That is what is transpiring with Timothy at Corinth. Timothy is continuing to carry a spiritual legacy that Paul has already begun. Spiritual sons and daughters are meant to continue to carry the legacy of spiritual fathers who have come before them.

Don't Do It Your Way

Many times when you begin to talk about imitating, people think that it diminishes individuality. Nothing is further from the truth. We are simply saying that you don't do things according to your flesh. The self-centered, egotistical, and arrogant attitude of the song made famous by Frank Sinatra that says, "I did it my way," doesn't work in the kingdom of God. This type of thinking is simply incompatible with God's Kingdom.

I remember as a young man there was a secular song that was very popular and the premise of the song was, "It's my way or the highway." This line of thinking is the epitome of human arrogance and pride. Unfortunately, there are many believers who possess this attitude. They are unwilling to continue a legacy, and as a result they start over on a new path. They were intended to continue a trail rather than start a new one. Don't do it your way; do it the way God ordained. Continue legacy! Be willing to pick up the ball and run where spiritual fathers have already blazed a trail.

Paul pours his knowledge, wisdom, and anointing into Timothy and then sends him to Corinth to continue his work. It was Timothy's work, but it was also a continuation of the work of Paul. The trail that had been started by Paul was to continue to be traveled by Timothy. The very door that was opened to Timothy at Corinth was as a result of Paul. Sons will be able to go through doors to which they didn't hold keys as they are faithful to simply follow the trail that has been set before them. There has already been a trail made and doors have already been opened; simply be faithful to continue down that path.

Glory to Glory

It was never the plan, purpose, or intent of God for there to be momentum loss from generation to generation. However, this is exactly what has happened. Why? It is because upcoming generations have felt it necessary to forge their own way rather than continue in the ways of their fathers. It is the desire of God that we go from glory to glory and from faith to faith. This comes as a result of one generation using the stopping point of the previous generation as their starting point. This is the way it was always designed to be. When we live this way we continue to go higher and higher.

Dr. Bill Hamon said this, "Lord, if I don't do anything else in my life or ministry, I want to create a platform for my children." This idea is continuing legacy. Today Dr. Hamon has three children who all serve God in ministry—continuing the legacy of his life and ministry. He also has hundreds of spiritual sons and daughters that are doing the same. This is the true heartbeat of all natural fathers and legitimate spiritual fathers. Likewise, the true heartbeat of spiritual sons is to continue the legacy of those who have gone before them.

We all need to pick up the ball and run with a spiritual legacy. I understand that some may not have a natural spiritual legacy to follow. If you don't have a natural godly legacy, find a godly legacy to which you can link yourself, grab the ball, and run with it.

Joined to Legacy

In 2 Kings 18, we find the account of Hezekiah beginning to reign as King of Judah. Hezekiah becomes King at the relatively young age of twenty-five. He did not have a good example set before him; he did not have a godly heritage. His father sacrificed his brother. His grandfather was a good man, but had no spiritual impact on the nation. His great-grandfather was unfaithful to God. His great-great-grandfather worshiped idols. His great-great-great-grandfather brought judgment by killing the High Priest who dared to speak against his evil. His great-great-great-great-grandfather was the grandson of Ahab and Jezebel and was an evil man. His great-great-great-great-great-grandfather abandoned God. However, Hezekiah never allowed a lack of recent, and not so recent, righteous family legacy to keep him from continuing a spiritual legacy.

Hezekiah actually turns things around in Judah. He removes idol worship and breaks down the altars of Nehushtan, the bronze serpent Moses created that was worshiped as a god. He totally revolutionized Judah. Hezekiah trusts God and sees continued victory due to the changes he makes.

This is how Hezekiah did it: he found the closest thing he could find to a godly spiritual legacy and continued it. The closest thing he could find was David. Hezekiah set it in his heart to link himself to David and continue that lineage. No one has a family line as rough as Hezekiah and if he could find a legacy to link to and continue a righteous line, there is hope for everyone.

Hezekiah says, "David was righteous. I will join myself to his legacy and continue in those ways." Hezekiah essentially claims David as his spiritual father and picks up and continues his legacy. Hezekiah begins to rip down idols and restore Israel to worship the Lord. He continues the legacy of David and runs with the ball.

Inside of Hezekiah's choice to continue legacy he finds incredible rewards. I believe these are the same rewards that we can reap as we are faithful to follow and continue a spiritual legacy. Let's take a look.

The Presence of the Lord

2 Kings 18:7 records, "The Lord was with him." The sweet presence of Almighty God was with Hezekiah as he continued the legacy of David. Inside of His presence there is peace no matter the circumstance. Inside of His presence there

is joy unspeakable. The very presence of God is released into the life of Hezekiah as he continues the legacy of David. It was David who said this about the presence of the Lord, "In Your presence is fullness of joy; At Your right hand are pleasures forevermore" (Psalms 16:11).

In His presence, there are pleasures and joy. I believe that Hezekiah experienced this same thing. Not solely because that's who God is, but rather that is the way that David experienced God. Hezekiah is able to experience the presence of God in the same way that David did because he links himself to David. God reveals Himself to Hezekiah in the same manner that He reveals Himself to David.

When you continue a legacy you get the benefit of knowing the Father God in the same way of those who go before you. You have the opportunity to discover God for yourself, but a portion of that is discovering Him in the same fashion of your spiritual lineage.

Prosperity

We see in 2 Kings 18:7, "He prospered wherever he went." The word *prosper* here means to have success. David is not a failure. Although he makes some mistakes, when David puts his mind to do something, he accomplishes it. Whenever Hezekiah links himself to the legacy of David, he experiences the same success of David. Be careful to whom you link yourself because if they are not successful, it will be difficult for you to succeed. However, if they have a great deal of success and you are a son truly linked to them, you will experience great success.

Everything flows from the head down. If you want to operate under an anointing, then get under that anointing. If you want your family to be together, get under a spiritual father who has their family together. God desires great success for His children. Spiritual fathers also desire great success for their sons and daughters.

I don't believe that God releases this success just so you can be successful, but rather so He can be glorified. Paul declares, "No flesh should glory in His presence" (1 Corinthians 1:29). That which God does within our lives is not for the purpose of self-exaltation; it is not about the glorification of our flesh. When God does something in your life it isn't simply for you; it is so that He can be glorified.

I believe that believers, Christians, should prosper more than anyone else on the face of the planet. Why? So they can give glory to God for what He has done. Don't buy into the lie that God wants you sick, broke, and unsuccessful. Neither should you accept the lie that he receives some sort of glory when a believer is in that condition. I, as a father, would find no joy in my children being at the bottom of society. As a matter of fact, we have a promise from God that he will make us the head and not the tail, above ONLY and not beneath (Deuteronomy 28:13). God wants you to have great success; He wants you to be above and not beneath.

You circumvent being unsuccessful if you are living according to biblical principle. David lived according to biblical principle and was blessed and prospered. Hezekiah continues this pattern; he restores the Law in the land and was blessed and prospers. He has great success! Hezekiah prospers in everything.

Walking in Victory

2 Kings 18:7 says, "He rebelled against the King of Assyria and did not serve him." King Ahaz, the father of Hezekiah, the King of Judah, strikes a deal with the King of Assyria, Sargon. The deal is this: as long as Ahaz gives money to Sargon, Assyria would not attack Judah. Not long after Hezekiah ascends to the throne, Sargon dies. In his place, Sennacherib rises up and becomes King of Assyria. At this time Hezekiah says, "I will no longer pay tribute to you Sennacherib." In other words, "I'm not giving you any more of what belongs to us." What does Sennacherib do? The armies of Assyria begin to march on Judah with hostile intent. You better believe that when you break ties with the enemy, he's going to come looking for vengeance. Sennacherib marches against Judah and begins to make threats. The prophet Isaiah gives a word concerning the fate of Sennacherib and the Assyrian army:

> *"Therefore thus says the LORD concerning the king of Assyria: 'He shall not come into this city, nor shoot an arrow there, nor come before it with shield, nor build a siege mound against it. By the way that he came, by the same shall he return; and he shall not come into this city,' says the LORD. 'For I will defend this city, to save it For My own sake and for My servant David's sake.'" (Isaiah 37:33-35).*

In this passage of Scripture, the prophet Isaiah begins to declare a word from God concerning the upcoming conflict with Assyria. He says Assyria will not come into the city, they will not even shoot an arrow, and that God will defend the city and save it. He finishes it by saying that He does this for His own sake and "for My servant David's sake." For my servant David's sake! What an incredible statement from an all-powerful God. David is not the current king in Judah; he hasn't even been alive in hundreds of years. What does David have to do with this? It's simple. Hezekiah is the spiritual heir of David in the earth at this time, and God moves powerfully because of David. There are hundreds of years between David and Hezekiah, but Hezekiah is continuing the legacy of David. Because of David, God is going to defeat Sennacherib and the armies of Assyria, and He does just that. The angel of the Lord goes into the camp of the Assyrians and destroys one hundred eighty-five thousand Assyrian soldiers in the middle of the night. Sennacherib and his army turn around and go home and never assault Judah again!

The Blessing Trumps the Curse

The father of Hezekiah worships idols; he bows down to graven images. Shouldn't Hezekiah be in defeat rather than victory because of the sin of his father? After all, God visits the sins of the fathers upon the children unto the third and fourth generation (Exodus 20:5). Why would God fight for Hezekiah when the sins of his father are so great? It is because generational blessings will always trump a generational curse.

Many people have put more faith in the curse than the blessing. God's blessing is stronger than any curse that we are due. Praise God for His mercy and grace. Hezekiah linked himself to the legacy of David, and he received the blessing of that legacy rather than the cursed lineage of his father. Realize that when you join yourself to a godly spiritual heritage you receive of the blessing of that lineage and curses are broken off you and your family. Hallelujah!

Part of the blessing of Hezekiah's spiritual legacy is this: God will defeat the enemy because of the faithfulness of David. Due to the spiritual lineage to which Hezekiah is linked, he receives victory; he doesn't have to fight the battle. He has already won because of his spiritual heritage.

Reaping Victory After Victory

When you join yourself to a spiritual legacy, there will be battles that you don't have to fight because of the history of the legacy. Not only did God defeat the Assyrians for the sake of Hezekiah's spiritual father David, the Bible also says that Hezekiah had victory against the Philistines. We know this was David's primary adversary during his lifetime.

Hezekiah reaps in a field where he had not sowed. Sons receive victories simply because of the history of their fathers and the fighting that they have already done—the victories they have already won. We can reap where we have not sown, but our fathers first sowed there. I don't expect to have to fight the same battles my father fought. Why? He has already defeated that enemy and it's now dead on the trail. There's no need to resurrect a defeated enemy. If he's been defeated, then he's been defeated. Hezekiah didn't have to fight the battle again because David had already gained victory over the Philistines. It was already finished! When we receive the adoption into the family of God, the struggle against death and sin is finished because Jesus already won that battle. You inherit the victories of your fathers.

It is a good thing to follow spiritual legacy. If for no other reason, you get to avoid fighting battles that have already been won. I have seen my generation fighting battles that have already been won simply because they failed to link themselves to a legacy. Some have believed they are so individual, so special, that it is necessary for them to forge their own path. This only results in failure to receive victory and prosperity that are already present and available. The unfortunate outcome is that many retrace steps that have already been made. If this has been you, I encourage you to stop going in circles and move forward.

Keep Following

We, as a generation, must make a choice to follow those who have come before us. To imitate them as they have imitated Christ. To honor, obey and respect them. As we do this, the rewards that we reap are beyond our wildest imagination.

CHAPTER 7
UNITY AND SYNERGY

When the Day of Pentecost had fully come they were all with one accord in one place. And suddenly there came a sound from heaven, as of a rushing mighty wind, and it filled the whole house where they were sitting. Then there appeared to them divided tongues, as of fire, and one sat upon each of them. And they were all filled with the Holy Spirit and began to speak with other tongues, as the Spirit gave them utterance (Acts 2:1-4).

In Charismatic and Pentecostal circles, this is a familiar passage of Scripture which gives the account of the early Church receiving the baptism of the Holy Spirit. Jesus tells the disciples to go tarry in Jerusalem until they are endued with power from on high. They are obedient and receive. Once again we see how receiving the promise is predicated by obedience. One hundred twenty people in the Upper Room receive the infilling of the Holy Ghost and power.

Peter goes into the street and begins preaching. As a result, three thousand people are born again in a moment. That's some incredible power! That's some anointed preaching! That's the manifestation of the Holy Spirit. I believe God desires to do these same things in the earth today.

91

There is something very specific that allows them to see this kind of power, this kind of authority, and this kind of fruit. It is found in an English phrase that is translated from one Greek word. The English phrase is "with one accord," and the Greek word it is derived from is *homothymadon*. The word literally means with one mind and with one passion. This word is unique and has ten of its eleven biblical uses found in the book of Acts. Is it a coincidence that possibly the most powerful church to ever walk the face of the planet was a church with one mind and one passion? God's power can always be found where there is unity.

God Blesses Unity

Behold, how good and how pleasant it is for brethren to dwell together in unity! It is like the precious oil upon the head, running down on the beard, the beard of Aaron, running down on the edge of his garments. It is like the dew of Hermon, descending upon the mountains of Zion; for there the LORD commanded the blessing—Life forevermore (Psalm 133:1-3).

David says that it is good for the brethren to dwell together in unity. He goes on to say it is like the "precious oil upon the head." David, under direction of the Spirit of God, compares unity to oil. We have already established in this book that oil is a signifier of the anointing of God. As a matter of fact the word translated "oil" is the Hebrew word *shemen* which means anointing. The psalmist compares unity to oil. Unity will always produce anointing.

When spiritual sons work with spiritual fathers there is unity. The unity of spiritual fathers and sons produces anointing. God will command His blessing where there is unity and anointing. If we are united, we will be anointed. If we are not united, there will be no anointing.

We Need Each Other

We have to come to this realization: we need each other. Sons need fathers and fathers need sons. A son without a father is not a son; he is illegitimate and does not receive blessing. A father cannot be a father without a son. That is the very thing that makes him a father—the presence of heirs—the presence of seed. We need each other in order to fulfill our God-given roles.

Not only do sons need fathers, but they need their brothers, too. My natural brother, Micah, and I work together on a continual basis. Our ministries and jobs are so interconnected that one of us cannot fulfill the fullness of what we need to do without the other. We need each other to fulfill our destiny. One generation needs another generation to fulfill the purposes of God. It takes more than one generation to fulfill God-given destiny. Therefore, generations have to be in unity to see the purposes of God fulfilled in the earth.

Joined Together

Romans 12:5 declares that we are one body and members of one another. Once again we need each other. It is fascinating that of everything to which we as the Church could be compared, we are compared to a body. Each individual body part needs the rest of the body. My brain, as intricate and fascinating as it is, is useless and of no good unless it is connected to the rest of my body. My arm is very unique. There is not another arm in the universe like my arm. However, once you remove my arm from the rest of the body, it becomes one hundred percent useless. It is unique, but useless.

I have found that many believers like to be unique, but disconnected from the rest of the body. My brain tells my arm what to do. The arm is unique, but must be obedient to the brain. If my arm is disobedient to the head of my body, then it is useless. My arm must be submissive to my brain. It cannot just do whatever it wants to do. If my arm attempted to function independently of my brain, it would indicate that something is dysfunctional with my arm. Likewise, if we are independent of the rest of the body, independent of spiritual fathers, then something is dysfunctional.

Unfortunately, there are many people who want to be an arm which is not connected to the rest of the body. My arm has to be attached to the rest of the body in order to be functional. This is why it is so important that we are linked with brothers, and we are obedient to spiritual fathers in our lives. If we are not connected, we will not be fruitful. We will not be productive.

The Danger of Being Disconnected

In May of 1962, there was a young man who had his right arm severed from his body while trying to "hop a train." This young man's arm was put on ice and within four hours doctors were working feverishly to attempt to reattach the arm; the operation was a success and the arm was reattached. After extensive rehabilitation, the young man was able to use his arm to its full capability. This was the first successful limb reattachment surgery to ever be conducted.

Praise God for the medical technology we have today. However, this isn't about medicine. I simply use that story to illustrate that if you have been disconnected, you can get reconnected. As a matter of fact, you must get reconnected. If not, you will cease to flourish. If a body part stays disconnected long enough, that body part will die; it cannot be reattached. Don't risk your part of the body dying. Get connected. We can do more together than we will ever be able to do alone.

Synergy

Synergy is defined as the working together of two things to produce a result greater than the sum of their individual effects. I recently read a story about a horse pulling contest where the horses were hooked to weighted sleds. The horse who pulled the most weight would win. The first place winner pulled four thousand five hundred pounds. The second place winner pulled four thousand pounds.

Someone at the competition decided it would be interesting to see what would happen if the horses were yoked together. How much weight could they pull? The horses were yoked together and they pulled twelve thousand pounds of weight on the sled. This is a perfect picture of the principle of synergy. When the horses were put together they pulled THREE TIMES the weight they could pull individually.

Your leaders and fellow laborers are worth more to you than you know. Through the principle of synergy, we will accomplish more together than we can alone. Your output multiplies when you are linked to a body, to a father, to a brotherhood. These people don't simply add to you, they multiply you. You have multiplied effectiveness when you are joined to the body—when you are joined and jointed to spiritual authority.

The reason that the law of synergy works in the natural is because it was a spiritual law first. Natural laws are reflective of spiritual laws that God established at the beginning. The principle of synergy, multiplied effectiveness, is a Kingdom principle. The Bible says if one can put a thousand to flight, two can put ten thousand (Deuteronomy 32:30). When we begin to work together instead of against each other we can accomplish so much more. Sons should cease attempting to work against fathers; they should be submissive and work with spiritual authority. You will be more effective if you are willing to work with the spiritual authority in your life.

> *I planted, Apollos watered, but God gave the increase. So then neither he who plants is anything, nor he who waters, but God who gives the increase. Now he who plants and he who waters are one, and each one will receive his own reward according to his own labor. For we are God's fellow workers; you are God's field, you are God's building (1 Corinthians 3:6-9).*

Paul talks about synergy in this passage of Scripture. Paul plants the seed, Apollos waters the seed, and God gives the increase. This is a picture of synergy between brothers and between man and God. We are co-laborers: fathers and sons, sons and brothers, and God and man. Paul says that we are God's fellow workers. The phrase "fellow workers" is the Greek word *synergos*. It is where we get our English word "synergy." Coincidence? I think not. Paul understood the power of synergy. This is why Paul can so confidently say in Philippians 4:13, "I can do all things through Christ who strengthens me."

Paul understands that when he works in synergy with God and the rest of the body of Christ nothing is impossible. He understands that one and one does not equal two. In the spirit, one and one equals multiplied fruit and effectiveness. It is not addition; it is multiplication.

It Takes More than One

As I have already stated in this chapter, it takes more than one generation to accomplish the plans and purposes of God. Think about it. We see this demonstrated in the Bible. From the time Adam falls, the entire plan and purpose of God is primarily to redeem man back to relationship with God and restore that which was lost. Does this happen in Adam's generation? No. Does it happen in Noah's time? No. Does it happen during Abraham's life? No. Does it happen during the time of David? No, not even David, the man after God's own heart.

These men are all faithful to fulfill God's purposes in their generation. They do their part and then pass the torch to those coming behind them. The Bibles says of David, "After he had served his own generation by the will of God, fell asleep, was buried with his fathers and saw corruption" (Acts 13:36). After David serves his purpose, he dies. Is the fullness of what God wanted fulfilled? No. Why isn't it fulfilled? It is because it requires more than one generation. David has a part to play in the "big picture," but his purpose is not the culmination of all things.

There are forty-two generations from Abraham to Jesus (Matthew 1:17). Forty-two generations to see the fullness of what God had already deemed His plan. God uses generations, not a generation. It's all about synergy. Generations accomplishing more together than they can alone. The purpose of God is being fulfilled from generation to generation. The purpose is fulfilled from spiritual father to spiritual sons and daughters. However, God is always working on a bigger picture that carries from generation to generation. This is why we must have synergy and unity between generations. We, as sons, must have unity and synergy with spiritual fathers in order to continue to see the purposes of God manifested once the spiritual fathers have fulfilled their earthly purpose.

The Enemy of Unity

In Proverbs 6:16-19, Solomon, the wisest man to ever live, gives us a list of things that God hates. He goes on to say the seventh is an abomination. What is the seventh? Is it pride? No. Is it lying? No. Is it shedding innocent blood? No. Is it devising wicked plans? No. Is it running toward and being given to evil? No. The thing that God says is an ABOMINATION is sowing discord among the brethren. It's being one who stirs strife in the kingdom of God. The Father takes this very seriously.

Satan will do everything within his power to sow strife between spiritual sons, spiritual fathers, and brothers in the faith. Why? It keeps the anointing from flowing and it keeps synergy, multiplied effectiveness, from becoming reality. **Strife sown into relationships within the body of Christ prevents destiny from being realized.**

How does the enemy sow strife? He causes us to be offended with one another. This ultimately leads to us talking about one another in an ungodly manner. Solomon said that evil is on the lips of an ungodly man like a burning fire

(Proverbs 16:27). If you want to be godly, be mindful that evil and corrupt speech is not coming out of your mouth. The ungodly man can't keep from seeking and talking about evil. He will speak negatively about spiritual leadership and other members of the body of Christ. This type of individual will separate members of the body. They will bring division and discord. They will cause more harm to seeing God's Kingdom established than they will good.

Solomon says, "The whisperer separates the best of friends" (Proverbs 16:28). The word "whisperer" literally means chatterer. My father always quoted this passage from Proverbs to me. He would tell me and my siblings, "In the abundance of words there is strife" (Proverbs 10:19). Sometimes you are better to not say anything at all. Know when to speak and when to stay quiet about situations. If something needs to be said, talk to the person with whom you have the issue or go to legitimate spiritual authority. Speak with someone who can resolve the situation. Above all, seek restoration and reconciliation.

In our modern culture today, we must realize that it's not only that which we literally articulate with our mouths, but what we type and post, also. Before you text, post, or tweet, examine the motive of your heart and be honest with yourself. Is that which I am typing true, noble, right, pure, lovely, admirable, excellent or praiseworthy? Are these things that should be discussed? Make sure you ask these questions before you press "send." The Bible says that the act of sowing discord is an abomination. I don't want to act in an abominable way. Therefore, I am going to watch what I say, type, and do. I refuse to operate in a way that God calls an abomination; I don't want to be an unfaithful son. I want to propagate unity and synergy.

Walk In Love

In his Epistle to the Colossians, Paul told them, "Make allowance for each other's faults, and forgive anyone who offends you" (Colossians 3:13). I have found that most discord is based in offense. Offense is present when there is a lack of mercy, grace, and love. I am thankful that others had mercy on me when I fell short. If we are honest, we would admit that we all have said and done things to offend others. Are we not thankful that Jesus, as the embodiment of mercy and grace, forgave us? We should, in turn, forgive others because we have been forgiven.

When you forgive you walk in love. This is what Paul told the church in Colossae. He told them to clothe themselves in love which is the key to overcoming offense. Jesus told His disciples that the world would know we are His disciples in that we have love for one another. He did not say that we would be known as His disciples because we love Him, but rather that we love each other. You do not present yourself as a true son, a true disciple, when you hold offense against your brother. Why? It is because you are not walking in love. We must love one another. When you love your brother, you will walk in unity. When we, as sons, love, honor, and obey our spiritual fathers we will walk in perfect harmony, bound together for the purposes of God.

It is not talent that brings anointing; it is unity. It is not merely hard work that brings about lasting generational effectiveness; it is synergy. Hard work is important, and talent is a good thing to possess; however, these things alone are useless without unity and synergy. As a son, allow your life to be one that is a showcase of unity and synergy.

CHAPTER 8
SPIRITUAL IDENTITY

Identity—the condition of being oneself, and not another.

To do what God has called you to do, you must have a proper understanding of who you are. You must have a proper identity. God has an identity to release that is uniquely you. Without receiving a true godly identity, you will flounder in life trying to figure out who you are while never hitting the mark and never seeing the full realization of your potential. If you don't know who you are, you don't realize what you are supposed to do and who you are supposed to be. Without this knowledge of your true identity, you will be unsuccessful in life and your calling.

In the world today, we have had a problem with identity theft. People literally have had their identities stolen, purchases made in their name, and debt accumulated in their name all because someone perverted and stole their identity. This continues to happen around the world on a daily basis.

Likewise, the enemy has attempted to steal the identity of people since the very beginning of time. Why has satan done this? He understands that if he can steal or pervert your identity he can control you. Then satan can get you to live up to something that was never yours in the beginning. There are many believers today who have assumed an identity that was never intended for them.

We have all seen commercials touting services that keep your identity safe and prevent fraud. The greatest form of identity protection we can have in the spirit realm is to truly know what our identity is as believers. We must understand who we are and what we are called to do in the world. We need to receive the true identity that was intended for us before the foundation of the world. Identity is released and imparted from our heavenly Father and spiritual fathers that God has placed in our lives.

Father: The Identity Giver

When we break down natural identity to its most basic identifier, you are either male or female. This is the baseline of all natural identity. The reason you are either male or female is because of your father. Scientifically, the determining factor of your gender is whether an X (male producing) or Y (female producing) sperm reaches and fertilizes the mother's waiting egg. The female egg does not determine your gender, but rather what the father gives. As we have said, the natural is a mirror of the spiritual. The biggest determining factor of your identity is what the father gives. As it is in the natural, so it is in the spirit.

All identity comes from a father. This is obviously true of us as Christians who receive our identity from Father God. You were born a sinner—born into a sin-filled world, but that was never your intended identity. If you are a believer, "sinner" is not your current identity. You are the righteousness of God in Christ Jesus (2 Corinthians 5:21). Your true identity is righteousness. That is not something you will be one day, but something you are right now, at this moment. You ALREADY ARE (present tense) the righteousness of God in Christ Jesus.

The enemy still tries to convince believers that they are sinners. Why does he do this? He does it in order to make us sin. If the accuser can convince you that you are something that you are not, you will act like that thing. The good news is that everything satan says is a lie. You are not a sinner; you are the righteousness of God in Christ Jesus. Your identity comes from your Father who is in heaven. He has already declared what you are. Don't believe the lie from the enemy.

This is the baseline of Christian identity. You are the righteousness of God in Christ. However, that is not the end of your identity. I am a male because of what my father supplied during the reproductive process, but I am not only a male. There is much more to who I am than just being male. That is not the end of my identity. You being the righteousness of God is not the end of your identity; it is the beginning. Father God supplied that seed, and you received Jesus' righteousness when you experienced the new birth.

As we have stated, the new birth is not the end of the journey; it is the beginning. This is only the root of my identity, not the end of it. God has placed inside of each one of us unique talents, abilities, and gifts. All of these things are part of the identity within us. However, these can lie dormant without someone to spark them and call those things forth.

My father supplied seed determining my baseline identity of being a male. Moreover, he continued to pour into my life after I was born and as I grew up. He continued to speak into my life.

He continued to teach and train me. All of these things released identity into my life to form me into the man I am today. Father God provided a seed for us to be the righteousness of His son, Jesus. The Father has also planted the seed of spiritual fathers in our lives to continue to release identity to us. Spiritual fathers are here to speak into our lives, to teach us, to train us, and to see us molded in the identity that heaven has for us.

Natural Identity vs. Spiritual Identity

Gideon is from the weakest clan in all of Israel. It's even worse than that: he is the runt of the litter. He is the smallest of the small and the weakest of the weak. When we meet him in the Bible he is threshing wheat in the wine press. Wheat is not meant to be threshed in a wine press; it is counterproductive. Wheat is to be threshed on the threshing floor; it is threshed in open places. This allows the wind to carry away the chaff while the grain falls to the ground to be easily harvested. There is no wind in the winepress.

Gideon is in this location because he is afraid; he is hiding like a coward. He is living up to being the weakest of the weak. Gideon is living up to the reputation that his natural identity has placed upon him. The Midianites are oppressing Israel, and Gideon is acting in fear by attempting to hide. Something very interesting happens when the Angel of the Lord appears to Gideon and speaks to him: "The Lord is with you, you mighty man of valor!" (Judges 6:12).

What? There is nothing mighty or valorous about Gideon. The exact opposite is true. Gideon is behaving in a weak and fearful manner. I probably would have said, "Gideon! Stop being a coward and do something about your current situation. Don't be a wimp." The entire reason Gideon is acting like a coward is because the identity to which he has come into agreement is based on natural circumstances. Yes, he may have been from the weakest clan, and he may have appeared to be the weakest member. He certainly was acting in that manner. However, God had planted a different identity inside of him. The Lord didn't make Gideon to be weak, wimpy, or a coward; He called Gideon a warrior.

Your natural lineage, your natural history, and your natural identity are irrelevant when it comes to the calling and identity that God has given you. God changes the name of an old man named Abram to Abraham so that his identity could be changed, and he could become the father of many nations. God calls those things that are not as though they were (Romans 4:17). God doesn't give you a spiritual identity and calling because of what you are in the natural. He gives you a calling, destiny, and spiritual identity despite your natural identity.

Gideon goes on to subdue and conquer the Midianites. The weakest of the weak becomes the mightiest of the mighty. The one who no one believes could do anything effectively leads the army in victory over the oppressors. This was all realized because Gideon refused to let his natural identity get in the way of a spiritual identity God released in his life. Your identity in the spirit will always trump what you are in the natural.

Fulfill Your Purpose

Everything placed inside of you, everything you are, and the things that make up your identity were put there for you to fulfill a purpose. Success is measured many ways today; money, fame, power, and ability are the things the world uses as their measuring stick. Understand that these things by themselves are not success. They may be a part of success, but they are not the fullness of it. Success is when you fulfill your purpose. Identity is given for the reason of fulfilling that purpose. If you don't know who you are, you can never do what you are called to do.

Part of the identity of Jesus' twelve disciples is to have power over unclean spirits and heal all kinds of sickness and disease. When Jesus proclaims this to them He gives them power to perform (Matthew 10:1). This power Jesus speaks of is a type of authority and jurisdiction. However, I also believe it was an identity. All authority comes from identity. The reason a law enforcement official has the authority to enforce law is due to the identification that they carry. Without identification, there is no authority. Without understanding who you are and what you have been called to do, you will do nothing. Purpose will be left unfulfilled.

There is a driving force in mankind to be relevant and be remembered; we strive to make an impact. The reality is if you fulfill your purpose, you will make an impact. If you accomplish the part that you are called to do, you will be remembered. I don't believe that Peter, James, and John conducted their ministry with the motivation of being famous and remembered. They were simply confident in who they were, their identity, and fulfilled their purpose. Stop trying to do everything and simply play the part that God has called you to play. How do you find that part? Know who you are. Know the identity God placed inside of you. How do you know who you are? Submit yourself to the voice of a spiritual father.

Spiritual Fathers and Identity

I believe that your identity not only comes from the Heavenly Father, but it also comes from spiritual fathers that God has placed in the earth. God has placed this leadership in the earth to release identity into sons and daughters. The reality is that God has put spiritual fathers in the earth as an extension of Himself. This leadership is not His replacement, but rather works in conjunction with Him to release His will, mind, and plans into the Church and to sons and daughters. Spiritual leadership, specifically the five-fold ministry, was placed into the earth "for the equipping of the saints" (Ephesians 4:11-12). Part of their equipping ministry is helping those within the body of Christ realize the identity God has given them. Spiritual fathers help to move us into proper alignment and receive an understanding of what the Heavenly Father has placed inside of us.

We have talked some about Samuel as a spiritual father when speaking into the life of Saul. However, Saul was not the only person whom Samuel addressed from the position of a father; he also spoke into the life of David.

By the time we get to 1 Samuel 16, the kingdom of Israel has been ripped from Saul. Samuel mourns. This is until God asks him how long he is going to cry over Saul. God tells him that He has already prepared another to replace Saul. The Lord tells Samuel to go to the house of Jesse the Bethlehemite; He actually says, "I have provided Myself a king among his sons" (1 Samuel 16:1). He had already done it. The identity of a king is locked inside of a young man; he just doesn't know it yet. Oftentimes, there is identity that God has placed inside of us, we just need a spiritual father to identify it and unlock it within us.

Samuel goes to the house of Jesse and all of his sons are paraded in front of the prophet. It is not Eliab. It is not Abinadab. It is not Shammah. Four more sons come before Samuel and none of them are anointed as king. Samuel is confused as to why none of the sons are called to be king. After all, God did tell him the next king would be found here at the house of Jesse. Samuel is informed there is one more son, a young shepherd named David. David comes before Samuel, and he is the one. God has already released the identity of kingship into this young shepherd. He didn't know about it until the voice of a spiritual father showed up in his life and began to pour oil over him.

David does not immediately begin operating in this identity even though God had already placed it inside of him. There is a prerequisite. David heeds the voice of Samuel—the voice of spiritual authority. He kneels before Samuel and gets under the oil that he is pouring out. David places himself under the anointing of the prophet Samuel. You can have all of the identity of a world changer and planet shaker locked inside of you, but until you put yourself under the anointing of spiritual headship it will remain dormant.

The kingship mantle lay dormant inside of David until he got under the oil of spiritual authority. After David gets under the oil, the Bible says, "The Spirit of the Lord came upon David from that day forward" (1 Samuel 16:13). There was an empowerment once the identity was released from a spiritual father. From this moment forward, David begins to act like a king and talk like a king. David operates under a kingship mantle.

Fast forward not long into the future of the life of David, and he finds himself delivering bread and cheese to the front lines of a battle with the Philistines. There he finds the giant Goliath calling for a champion of Israel to come and fight him. No one is answering the challenge. David steps up to the plate, as a king should do.

Understand during this time in history, this challenge should have been answered by a king. Saul should have fought Goliath, but Saul no longer had the mantle of the King of Israel. Saul is sitting in the throne, but is not really the one and true king. David has the mantle without a throne, while Saul has a throne without a mantle. David sets out to fight Goliath. He even stands up to Goliath for speaking ill and mocking Israel and Jehovah God. Once again, something Saul, as king, should have done.

If you went to Sunday school or had a picture Bible as a child, you know how this story ends. David defeats Goliath, and the Philistines are sent running for the hills. Why did David fight Goliath? It wasn't simply because Goliath was mocking God; it was because David was operating with the identity of a king.

Acting in this authority, this identity of kingship begins to push David toward ultimately sitting on the throne. The people begin to sing David's praises in the streets. They begin to realize that David could be the king of Israel. People begin to look at David differently because David knew his anointing and identity. He is propelled toward his ultimate destiny as King of Israel. Acting in the anointing of your prophetic identity will push you to the fullness of realizing that identity.

All of this begins in David's life by submitting himself to the oil—the anointing—of a spiritual father. Submit your life to the oil—to the anointing—of a spiritual father and become the fullness of what God has called you to be. It will cause you to receive your identity.

CHAPTER 9

THE JOURNEY: GILGAL

And it came to pass, when the Lord was about to take up Elijah into heaven by a whirlwind, that Elijah went with Elisha from Gilgal. Then Elijah said to Elisha, "Stay here, please, for the LORD has sent me on to Bethel." But Elisha said, "As the LORD lives, and as your soul lives, I will not leave you!" So they went down to Bethel. Now the sons of the prophets who were at Bethel came out to Elisha, and said to him, "Do you know that the LORD will take away your master from over you today?" And he said, "Yes, I know; keep silent!"(2 Kings 2:1-3).

In chapter 3 of this book, we talk about Elijah throwing his mantle on Elisha. This act is an invitation to sonship, an invitation to service, and an invitation to ultimately walk in the same office, mantle, and authority as Elijah. However, Elisha does not wear that mantle the next day, the next week, or even the next year. There is a great period of time between Elijah throwing the mantle on Elisha and Elisha receiving the double portion anointing.

Most scholars agree that Elisha served Elijah for at least ten years before he received the mantle of Elijah. Elisha had a journey to the double portion. I have found that there are many who want a double portion anointing, but not many who want a double portion journey. I have found many want to wear the mantle, but few are willing to endure the process. There is no other way to the double portion anointing other than the double portion journey—the journey of a spiritual son.

I have discovered in my life that there are no shortcuts in the kingdom of heaven. Yes, God can accelerate a process, but there is still the process. There is no quick way to receive the double portion that can only come from serving a spiritual father and from being mentored. Going through a prayer line, giving to certain ministers, reading books, watching Christian ministry television shows, and going to conferences cannot replace the path of sonship. Positioning yourself to receive the double portion takes time, dedication, and commitment.

We get a picture of this path—of this journey—as we take a look at the final journey that Elisha embarks on with Elijah. There is great significance in the journey they take and more specifically the locations mentioned in this account. This gives us a prophetic glimpse of the road—the journey—to the double portion anointing.

The place they begin is Gilgal which is a place of covenant and cutting. In Biblical narrative, one of the first instances of Gilgal being mentioned is located in Joshua 5. A bold, strong, and powerful generation has arisen from the children of Israel. However, before they can go forward and move into the fulfillment of prophetic words over their lives, they must first endure circumcision. Circumcision is a surgical procedure in which the foreskin is removed from a man's reproductive organ. This is not a procedure that men are joyfully anticipating. Circumcision involves a knife cutting away flesh in a sensitive area. It hurts. God instituted this procedure with Abraham as a sign of His covenant.

Covenant

In Genesis 17, God makes a covenant with Abraham. The Lord tells Abraham that He will cause exponential increase to come to his house. The way that this covenant is to be ratified is that Abraham and all in his house (and future generations) will be circumcised in the flesh. This was to be the sign of the covenant.

We know that today our hearts are circumcised at the time of salvation, and the outward sign of circumcision is no longer needed for covenant with God. However, the Old Testament is given for our example (Romans 15:4). Thus, we cannot simply ignore these things in the Old Testament and write them off as archaic, unnecessary, or pointless. There is spiritual and prophetic significance inside the act of circumcision. I do not believe it is some sort of coincidence that Elijah and Elisha start their journey at Gilgal. It reveals to us that sons have to live a life of covenant. Covenant is the place of origination for the double portion journey.

What is covenant? Covenant is an agreement between two parties based upon relationship; it is a formal and serious agreement. You don't enter into a covenant relationship with someone that you do not know or trust. The relationship between spiritual fathers and spiritual sons is to be a serious thing which must be born from relationship. You cannot have a spiritual father whom you are not in close relationship. Your favorite television minister cannot act as a spiritual father in your life because there is no relationship from which covenant can be birthed and acted upon. Covenant is not to be entered into lightly or flippantly.

I also believe that covenant is life-long. Just as our covenant with God is ongoing, so is our relationship with spiritual fathers. I have known those who bounce around from place to place, from authority to authority, from spiritual father to spiritual father. This is usually because when the moment of circumcision by the spiritual authority comes, they do not submit to the process. You will never receive the fullness of what God wants spiritual fathers to pour into your life if you refuse to live from a place of covenant. Covenant should be firmly established and unshakable.

Timothy, the spiritual son of Paul, understood the importance of covenant and endured with Paul through all situations and circumstances. On the other side of the coin you had Demas who traveled right alongside Paul. Demas saw great miracles. Demas heard great teaching. Demas saw demons cast out. I'm sure Demas even had the opportunity to serve Paul in the capacity of a spiritual son; however, Demas was not a person of covenant. Timothy would learn of this when Paul wrote to him, "...for Demas has forsaken me, having loved this present world, and has departed for Thessalonica" (2 Timothy 4:11).

Demas wasn't in it for the long haul. He wasn't a true son like Timothy. Demas left Paul, the one who had mentored him. Paul gave his life to train Demas, and Demas leaves him for Thessalonica, a city filled with opportunity, but also great wickedness.

Demas didn't value Paul, nor did he value the voice of a spiritual father in his life. When an opportunity to leave came, he didn't hesitate. He bolted. When something that he perceived as greater came along (Thessalonica), Demas departed. Don't chase opportunity. Worldly, fleshly opportunity comes and goes, but the opportunity to serve a spiritual father and receive a double portion is greater and more gratifying than anything the world can offer.

I think about how many opportunities Elisha may have had to leave Elijah, but he endured. There is no job, fame, or promise from man that could take me away from serving the authority God has placed within my life. Godly authority in the earth is a blessing. It's not always the easiest to submit, but I know that at the end of the day the reward is so much greater than anything man could give. These men—Timothy, Elisha, Joshua, and so many other sons throughout the Bible—were faithful to spiritual fathers in their lives. As sons, we must follow their example and be faithful to spiritual fathers.

Will you be Demas or will you be Timothy? Will you be Demas or will you be David? Everything that glitters isn't gold. Don't chase opportunity and forsake the leadership God has placed within your life. Endure the process and live a life of covenant.

The Cutting

Gilgal is a place of covenant, but it is also a place of cutting. The reality is that there was something in the lives of the sons of Israel that would alienate them from their prophetic promise. God's answer to this conundrum: a spiritual leader with a sharp edge. God tells Joshua to make flint knives

Sonship

and to cut away what is keeping the people from experiencing their divine destiny. Today, God still calls spiritual leadership to bring us to Gilgal moments where they cut away the things that are keeping us from the fullness of our potential and promise.

These Gilgal moments are sometimes painful. I think about the children of Israel who have just seen the Jordan part. They are victorious and feel like champions—like conquerors. They are finally moving forward to destiny after wandering in the wilderness for forty years. Then, God tells Joshua to pull out the knife and begin to cut on them. I can guarantee you that after the Gilgal moment they didn't feel like celebrating. They were hurting, they were sore, and they needed rest after this procedure. It was not enjoyable, but it was necessary to move forward.

My Gilgal Experience

I can remember Gilgal moments in my life. One specific time in my early days of preaching I can recall vividly. My father, Robert Gay, would always critique me after I had ministered. One night I ministered and felt particularly confident about the delivery of the message. People were touched, and I received many compliments. I felt as if I had finally arrived as a minister. I felt like I had crossed the Jordan, and I was moving forward to destiny. I remember thinking about how excited I was to sit down with my father and hear him praise how great the message was. I was wrong. I was about to be brought to Gilgal.

He started by acknowledging the good and that people were touched. For me, this was a victory. He then followed that up by pointing out some of the weaker aspects. He pointed out times when I sounded prideful and boastful and how I had gone over my time allotment. There were several other issues he brought up with my ministry that night. Ouch. It hurt in that moment. This was a sensitive area; this was my ministry. However, spiritual authority in my life pulled out the knife and cut in that area.

When I was ministering and preaching I felt like the children of Israel having crossed Jordan. But after crossing over, I had my Gilgal moment. This is only one of many Gilgals that I have endured. I wouldn't change a single one of them. There is not one time that I have allowed spiritual authority to speak into my life where I left regretting that decision. I certainly have questioned the cutting in that moment when the pain was fresh; however, I never regretted it once I had experienced the fruit wrought from the cutting process.

I can guarantee you that whenever the men of Israel went into their promised land, Canaan, not a single one regretted the cutting. As a matter of fact, they probably would have endured the circumcision one hundred more times to be standing in the fullness of what God had promised. One of the things required for them to possess Canaan was allowing Joshua, a spiritual father, to cut in a sensitive area. Today, part of the process of seeing the fullness of your destiny manifested is allowing spiritual leadership to cut in sensitive areas within your life.

From Love

When Joshua cut on the sons of Israel, it wasn't because he enjoyed causing them pain. He did not hate them; the exact opposite of this is true. Joshua loved these people so much that he was willing to pull out the knife and cut away. If Joshua had not cared, he would not have cut on them. When a spiritual father begins to cut in your life IT IS NOT abuse. So many miss out on this part of the process because the moment they begin to hurt a little bit, they view it as abuse and run away.

Now there are certainly some who call themselves "spiritual fathers" who have operated in abuse. I am not discounting legitimate instances of abuse by "leaders." If someone calling themselves spiritual leadership is only tearing down and is overly harsh, then we could possibly question their validity as a leader. True spiritual fathers work on the sensitive areas of our lives because they truly love us. These leaders—men and women of God—speak words of life, edification, and comfort into our lives. However, they are not afraid to correct, rebuke, and speak into our lives about our shortcomings and areas that need to be shown attention. These things are not done for our breaking, but rather our making.

Correction is a biblical concept. God Himself brings correction. The Bible declares, "Whom the LORD loves He chastens, and scourges every son whom He receives" (Hebrews 12:6). This is not exactly a verse that makes us want to shout and run around the sanctuary. However, it is in the Bible and in the New Testament, at that. I have found that the Lord chastens us in many ways. He teaches and corrects us through His Word and speaks to us during times of prayer. However, He also chastens through the voices of spiritual leadership in the earth. It's not one method or the other; it's all of them together. God uses several different methods to bring chastening to our lives.

The writer of Hebrews goes on to say, "But if you are without chastening, of which all have become partakers, then you are illegitimate and not sons" (Hebrews 12:8). Chastening, cutting, and allowing legitimate fathers to speak into the sensitive areas of our lives are an inescapable part of sonship. You cannot refute it, and walk in the promise. You cannot refute it and claim sonship. The Bible says if you refuse it then you are "illegitimate." The children of Israel couldn't refuse the circumcision and continue to Canaan. Circumcision is a prerequisite to destiny.

Embrace Gilgal

We learn from Scripture that from the time the Hebrews left Egyptian slavery until the conquest of Jericho, no men born in the wilderness had been circumcised. This meant that there were men as old as forty that now had to endure the knife; they endured the cutting away. A man twenty, twenty-five, thirty or forty years old could have chosen not to endure this procedure; however, they made a choice that it was worth it. Their destiny was worth it. Their purpose was worth it. Canaan was worth it. If they had made the choice that it wasn't worth it, they would have never seen Canaan and would have died in the wilderness. You also have a choice.

I have seen those who have made the wrong choice. They have been too prideful and arrogant to allow spiritual fathers to speak into their lives—to bring them to Gilgal. These people eventually forsook leadership and today are still wandering in the wilderness. How much untapped potential is in the pews of the world today because people who were called wouldn't endure Gilgal? Thankfully God is rich in mercy, and I believe that people will be given another opportunity. However, there is no short-cutting Gilgal. If you do not choose to embrace the place called Gilgal, you will never reach Canaan—you will never reach the promise. Embrace covenant. Embrace the cutting. Embrace Gilgal.

CHAPTER 10
THE JOURNEY: BETHEL

Then Elijah said to Elisha, "Stay here, please, for the LORD has sent me on to Bethel." But Elisha said, "As the LORD lives, and as your soul lives, I will not leave you!" So they went down to Bethel. Now the sons of the prophets who were at Bethel came out to Elisha, and said to him, "Do you know that the LORD will take away your master from over you today?" And he said, "Yes, I know; keep silent!" (2 Kings 2:2-3).

After Elijah and Elisha depart from Gilgal, they head for their next destination, Bethel. After encountering and going through the place of cutting—the place of submission—they continue on to Bethel. Bethel is an incredibly historic place in biblical history. Abraham builds an altar in Bethel and invokes the name of the Lord for the first time (Genesis 12:8), and the Ark of the Covenant was set up in Bethel (Judges 20:26-27). Arguably, the person most linked to Bethel is Jacob who would later be called Israel. Bethel is more pivotal to Jacob than any other person in biblical history. Inside the significance of Bethel to Jacob, we find the prophetic significance of Bethel to spiritual sons. Bethel is the place of encounter, dream, and identity. Bethel is also where selfishness dies.

The Bad Guy

When the Bible first mentions Jacob it is at the time of his birth. Jacob and his brother Esau struggle throughout their time in the womb, and when they are born Jacob is holding Esau's heel. For this reason, he was named Jacob which means "that supplants, that undermines, the heel." From the very time he is born, Jacob is labeled as a bad guy, the supplanter. In America, we even use the term "heel" to identify a dishonorable, dishonest, or just downright bad person. Jacob certainly lives up to his reputation in his early life.

Jacob is a scheming evil opportunist going so far as to manipulate his brother to sell his birthright and deceive his own father in order to get the blessing that goes with that birthright. Jacob was one distorted and warped individual. However, this was all pre-Bethel. Something happens to Jacob at Bethel that totally changes who he is. It goes to the very core of Jacob and completely revolutionizes his identity. He encounters God and a dream is released.

Encounter and Dream

After Jacob receives the blessing of his father Isaac, it enrages Esau. Jacob ends up fleeing to avoid the rage of his older brother. It is at this juncture that he ends up in a place that is unknown to him: Bethel. Jacob spends the night there and while he is sleeping, the Lord appears to him for the first time. In other words, Jacob has a real and authentic encounter with God for the first time in his entire life.

As the Lord is speaking to Jacob, he releases this promise—this dream into his life, "I am the Lord God of

Abraham your father and the God of Isaac; the land on which you lie I will give to you and your descendants" (Genesis 28:13). The place of encounter is the seedbed of destiny in the life of Jacob. The place of encounter, Bethel, is the seedbed of destiny in the life of spiritual sons. What do I mean when I say it is the seedbed of destiny? The place of encounter is where God begins to plant a seed in your spirit of what His plans and intentions are for your life.

The Lord releases a dream to Jacob when he is camped at Bethel. God tells Jacob that He is going to give this land to Jacob and to his descendants. The Lord plants a seed of destiny in the life of Jacob. He doesn't have descendants so this can't come into reality tomorrow, but He gives Jacob a vision of his future. I have found that most of the time the dream that God releases isn't for today; He releases a dream for a season down the road. It is yours to tend, much like a farmer who tends a seedbed. Be faithful with the dream He releases, and you will see it flourish.

This vision God releases is something that Jacob would never have dreamed on his own. This is something greater than any ambition that Jacob possessed. It's greater than any plan that Jacob had conjured. I want you to understand this: God's dream for your life is ALWAYS better than your plans. There is never an exception to this fact.

How fascinating is it that Elijah and Elisha go through this place on their final journey together—the same place where Jacob encountered God and received a dream for his life? I believe we see a prophetic picture communicating with us that in the time that Elisha served Elijah, Elisha encountered God in a real and authentic way just as Jacob did. During these times of encounter, Elisha sees a picture of what God wants to do in his life. He began to understand and know God's dream.

Understand that sonship isn't just about the cutting. It's not just about the rebuke. It's not just about serving. Sonship is about an ENCOUNTER! Sonship is about the DREAM! When you allow spiritual fathers to speak into your life it will allow you to encounter God in a way that you never have before. It will release a dream greater than you ever imagined. How can I be so sure of this? Jacob and Elisha experienced it! I have seen it too!

My Bethel Experience

When I was a young man the last thing on earth that I ever wanted to do was follow in the footsteps of my father. I didn't want to lead worship. I didn't want to preach. I didn't want to write books. I didn't want my "professional life" to look anything like his. Our family life was great and one that I always desired to emulate. However, I didn't want to have the same career path of my father.

It wasn't because I dislike my father; I love my father. It wasn't because I had issues with Christianity or God Himself; I love God and was delighted to be a believer. It essentially came down to this: I had a different plan for my life. My plan was to graduate from high school with an advanced placement program. After graduation, I would attend Florida State University where I would receive my law degree and become a lawyer.

Obviously, my life didn't take this course. If it had, I probably wouldn't be writing this book right now. It wasn't because I couldn't have, and it's not because there was anything wrong with my plan. My plan was a good thing, but it wasn't God's plan for my life. My dream was to be similar to attorney Jay Sekulow and defend the freedoms of Christians in the judicial arena. A great thing to do and something we need more of in society. God simply had a different plan for my life. My dream was good, but the God dream is always better than a good dream. His ways are so much higher and so much better.

As I have already detailed earlier in chapter 2 of this book, one of my first assignments I ever had in ministry was producing television. This was done simply from a place of obedience to authority in my life, not because I had always wanted to produce television. At the age of sixteen, I still had all of my plans as my first choice, but something began to change. I was about to receive His dream instead of my own.

As I allowed my father to speak into my life, not simply as Dad, but as the voice of spiritual authority in my life, things began to change. I can't nail down an exact moment, but I can remember the next two years set a course of encountering God repeatedly in ways that I had never previously experienced. The presence of the Lord was suddenly more real to me than it had ever been. It was in these moments—these times of encounter—that God began to release things into my life about which I had never dreamed. People that I greatly respected and admired began to declare things and speak things over my life that altered everything that I had ever thought about myself, my life, and my future.

I can remember times when I was alone in my unassuming office doing something that seemed menial (television editing) that God's presence would fill that small office and I would begin to look at life differently. It was as if I was seeing everything with different eyes. God spoke to me in these moments when no one else was around. Suddenly, the things I previously said were undesirous (preaching, teaching, and leading worship) became the things I desired to do most in my life. As the year 2003 closed, I was eighteen and had graduated high school; I was not on my way to Florida State University. I was on staff at our church, High Praise Worship Center, and was serving in ministry, something that I am still doing to this very day over a decade later.

My plan was good and my dream was good, but God's was better. I found this dream—this destiny—inside a place of encounter with the Spirit of the living God. What changed from the time that I was fifteen and sixteen that opened the door for this encounter? I certainly matured some. But in reality, a sixteen year old young man is still very immature. It wasn't that I was so mature or so advanced; it was this simple fact: I chose to embrace the voice of spiritual authority that God had placed in my life. I had encountered God before; however, once I made the choice to heed the voice of authority, it took me to Bethel. It made way for a new kind of encounter in my life.

Since then my life has never been the same. I know if you submit to authority and allow yourself to have a Bethel experience, you will never be the same either. Everything in your life will change.

A New Identity

Genesis 28 is not the only account of Jacob in Bethel. His next experience in this place literally shapes his future. Jacob has grown older. He now has wives, children, and a family. He still remembers the promise—the destiny—that God gave him. God is going to give him "the land on which you lie." This, of course, was the land of Canaan in which Bethel was located. Jacob hasn't seen the promise yet. He has been serving in the house of another man, his father-in-law Laban, for twenty years. He's simply been faithful even when Laban was unfaithful to him. God speaks to Jacob and tells him to return to Bethel. Jacob returns and his very identity is changed.

Then God appeared to Jacob again, when he came from Padan Aram, and blessed him. And God said to him, "Your name is Jacob; your name shall not be called Jacob anymore, but Israel shall be your name." So He called his name Israel (Genesis 35:9-10).

Names have a great deal of significance, more specifically the meaning of names. Jacob was called the supplanter and the heel. He was identified as the bad guy. However, in Bethel he is given a new identity. He is no longer Jacob, the bad guy. Jacob becomes Israel, which means "triumphant with God." God tells him, 'You are no longer the bad guy, you are victorious. You are no longer the supplanter; you are now triumphant.'

I have always found it intriguing that Jacob is beckoned to return to Bethel AFTER he has served in the house of Laban. Faithfully serving authority will open the door for God to pour more into you. Even if the authority is unfaithful, like Laban, God still honors your faithfulness. Laban was as unfaithful and scheming as they come. Jacob fell in love with Laban's daughter Rachel, and the father tells Jacob that if he will serve for seven years he can marry Rachel. Jacob fulfills his service and Laban pulls "the ole switcheroo." Laban gives away Rachel's older sister, Leah, to be wed, unbeknownst to Jacob. This is dysfunctional, deceptive, and just wrong.

However, Jacob still wants to marry Rachel after all of Laban's shenanigans. So, the father offers Rachel if Jacob will work for him for seven MORE years. There is no indication that Jacob complains; he is simply faithful. After seven years, Laban lives up to his end of the bargain, and Jacob marries Rachel. In the midst of unfaithfulness by a leader in the life of Jacob, he remains faithful. It is this lifestyle—the lifestyle of faithfulness—that opens the door for Jacob to experience another encounter in Bethel. In this encounter, God changes his name; the Lord releases the God-identity within Jacob's life.

God didn't change Jacob's name because He was more fond of the name Israel. In changing his name, there was a prophetic announcement that he was no longer the bad guy, the deceiver. God was announcing that everything that had been said about Jacob was past. He was saying that Jacob was no longer that which he had been associated and identified by others. God was declaring over Jacob, "You are not the heel. Israel, you are the one who is victorious! You've made it! You are now going to enter into what I promised you many years ago." Faithfulness always leads to a greater revealing of identity. Faithfulness always reveals another piece of the puzzle.

The Death of Self

The first instances of Jacob in the Bible reveal a portrait of a self-absorbed and self-centered man who is only concerned with himself and what he can get. My friend, selfishness is not a fruit of the spirit, yet Jacob exhibited it constantly. If we're honest, all of us in our flesh are a lot like Jacob. Human beings tend to be opportunist. Our flesh wants to look out for "number one" where our biggest concern is me, myself and I. From the time that Jacob leaves Bethel, he is a changed man. Something inside of his encounter with God caused the self-absorbed, self-centered version of Jacob to be annihilated. We can look no further than his reunion with his brother Esau to see this demonstrated.

Jacob essentially took everything from Esau. He took his birthright—the most valuable thing a son could have. When Jacob realizes he will see his brother for the first time in twenty years, he is obviously nervous. Jacob sends presents to Esau to try to quell any anger that may still be lingering. Jacob is quite surprised when Esau greets him with an embrace, and there is no animosity. Esau is not interested in causing Jacob great pain and bodily harm; his brother refuses the gifts that Jacob sent. He doesn't want anything from Jacob, but it doesn't end there.

> *If I have now found favor in your sight, then receive my present from my hand, inasmuch as I have seen your face as though I had seen the face of God, and you were pleased with me. Please, take my blessing that is brought to you, because God has dealt graciously with me, and because I have enough." So he urged him, and he took it (Genesis 33:10-11).*

Something has drastically changed in the life of Jacob. The self-serving guy is gone and has been replaced by a man who no longer wants to take from his brother, but rather give to him. What happened? Bethel happened. Jacob had an encounter.

Understand that God has always called for us to labor alongside other sons. It isn't just about you and spiritual authority. It's about serving the purposes of God. In order to do this, you will have to work with other spiritual sons and daughters. However, this cannot be accomplished while we are still self-oriented. This is one reason we must go to Bethel—to rid ourselves of selfishness and self-ambition in order to work with those to whom God has called us to labor: our spiritual brothers and sisters.

James and John Syndrome

James and John made a rather unusual request to Jesus. They asked if one may sit at His right hand and the other on His left in His glory (Mark 10:35-45). I've always read this and thought to myself, "What an odd request. I would simply be happy to be in His presence." The problem is not necessarily in the request that they make, but rather the heart condition that it reveals: selfishness and competitiveness. While I am certainly not questioning the faithfulness of James and John, you must remember that there are ten other guys who are traveling with Jesus—ten other disciples who are ministering with Him. Why should James and John be afforded these spots? Better yet, why are they concerned with this?

They are so concerned with being the greatest that they momentarily lose sight of what is most important. What is most important is living a lifestyle of a servant. Jesus emphasizes this with His response to them. Mark 10:43-44 says, "Whoever desires to become great among you shall be your servant. And whoever of you desires to be first shall be slave of all." Jesus says, 'Hey guys, if you want to be great, live the life of a servant *(author's paraphrase)*.'

If we are not careful, our vision to be successful and do everything that God has called us to do can turn to competitiveness. It can turn into a striving to be greater than someone else. This is exactly what happened to James and John. They were trying to prove themselves to others rather than resting in what God called them to do and simply doing their part. James and John had a role to fulfill, and it was obviously incredibly important. So why get caught up in the question of who is greatest? Simply do what you're called to do, and let self-centered and competitive thoughts die. Don't be one who is at odds with your brothers—with co-laborers—in the kingdom of God.

All the other disciples were angered when they heard James and John's request. Why? The request was all about self; it was all about James and John. It wasn't about serving others. It wasn't about serving Jesus. It wasn't about seeing people's lives changed. It was solely about them. If you are constantly absorbed with self, you need to have an encounter and let selfishness die. You will find yourself living in greater freedom, greater productivity, and greater joy when you let competitive and self-centered attitudes die.

Embrace Bethel

Jacob was competitive from the womb, trying to be the first born. Yet, something changes in the life of Jacob and he becomes this unselfish servant. What happened? Bethel happened.

131

In the place of encounter, all selfishness and self-ambition dies. You become generous and giving. When you have an encounter at Bethel you let the heart of the servant begin to take over your life. When you have an encounter at Bethel God releases destiny—He releases a dream in your life. Embrace the encounter. Embrace the dream. Embrace destiny. Embrace His identity for your life. Embrace Bethel.

CHAPTER 11
THE JOURNEY: JERICHO

Then Elijah said to him, "Elisha, stay here, please, for the LORD has sent me on to Jericho." But he said, "As the LORD lives, and as your soul lives, I will not leave you!" So they came to Jericho. Now the sons of the prophets who were at Jericho came to Elisha and said to him, "Do you know that the LORD will take away your master from over you today?" So he answered, "Yes, I know; keep silent!" (2 Kings 2:4-6).

When we begin to think about Jericho there is one very specific event that comes to mind: Joshua and the battle of Jericho. It is a story that I'm sure every Sunday school attending child has heard numerous times by the time they have reached adulthood. You may have even sung about how the "walls came a tumbling down" when Joshua fought the battle of Jericho. Memories of flannelgraph and puppets may race to your head. It's a classic story.

So what is the significance of Jericho? Why was this one of the places that Elijah and Elisha visited on that last fateful trip? How is Jericho relevant in the life of a spiritual son? If we can look a little way past the obvious account and look deeper, we will see that Jericho is the place where we pass the test and promise is fulfilled.

Testing the Heart

Moses is dead. That's how the entire book of Joshua starts. Moses is gone, and Joshua is now leading the Hebrews. Joshua and Caleb lived through the bondage of Egypt, and they saw the great miracles that God performed both during the Exodus and their time wandering the wilderness. They saw the generation before them complain their way out of destiny. Their parents, an entire generation, had to die in the wilderness because they couldn't stop complaining against God, against Moses, and generally against any type of authority or order.

This generation that Joshua is now leading has experienced and seen a lot. It is now their time to be "the ones." It is their turn to run with the proverbial ball. God has to make sure that this generation doesn't possess the same weakness or the same problem that the previous generation possessed. How does God determine this? God is going to test them.

Before they can enter into the promise that God has for them, they are going to encounter a gigantic test. The children of Israel encounter the first obstacle that stands between them and their promised land. You have to remember this land that was promised to Abraham, Isaac, Jacob, and their descendants had already been given to them and they are well aware of this fact. They have been told that Canaan belongs to them since they were young. The obstacle that stands between them and destiny is a city called Jericho.

Jericho is a fortress city that stands strong and mighty. More than likely, Jericho is more intimidating than any other city of the Bronze Age. This city that is so frightening has to be conquered in order for them to advance into the purpose that God has for the Hebrews. God has a plan that will not only bring victory if followed, but also allows the hearts of this generation to be tested.

God tells Joshua that all the men of war are to march around the city one time for six days. On the seventh day, they are to march around seven times, and the priests are to blow the trumpets. When the people hear the blasts of the trumpets they are to lift up a shout. Then and only then will the walls fall flat. Jericho can't be conquered by force or by any traditional means. It will be conquered by marching, shouting, and the blowing of trumpets. In all reality, it will be conquered by being obedient to what God has said. The marching and shouting were just the method God chose for victory to be established.

Joshua is the only one who gets this message from God; Caleb and the other Hebrews do not hear it. Joshua alone gets these instructions from God. Joshua, the spiritual authority in Israel, is given the battle plan for victory. He must now relay this to the people that he is leading.

I have often thought about Joshua having to give these instructions to the people. I've thought of him saying, "Ok, guys. I know that this city is huge, and for a lot of you, this is the first time you've ever even seen a city considering we've been in the wilderness for forty years. Some of you are seeing a wall for the first time in your life. It just so happens that the first one you see is gigantic. I've got some good news though.

God has given me the battle plan for us to have victory. It's simple. We march around the walls one time a day for six days. On the seventh day, we will march around seven times, and then our priests will blow trumpets and we will shout. Those gigantic, thick, and fortified walls are going to fall down when we shout, and we're going to be victorious. Oh wait, I almost forgot, the entire time we are marching, NO ONE UTTERS A WORD. You guys got it? Good! Let's go!"

Let's be honest, most Christians today would not respond very well to the instructions that Joshua gave the people. Today there would be responses like, "Well God didn't tell me that." We would also hear, "That Joshua is so controlling." We may even hear in some places, "Maybe we should get the board together and vote Joshua out as pastor of Israel. I never voted for him to begin with." This is the exact response that the previous generation had.

One day, Miriam is displeased at Moses' direction and said, 'Hey, God doesn't just speak to him' (Numbers 12:2, *paraphrased*). God didn't respond very kindly to this statement, and Miriam was struck with leprosy. The only reason she was healed was because of the humility and mercy of Moses to ask God to heal her. Even after she was healed, she became nothing more than a footnote in history for the rest of her life.

The reality is that we don't appreciate other people telling us what to do. The attitude is, "God speaks to me as well." This is what many people think. While I certainly believe that God speaks to each and every one of us, God speaks different things to different people. He releases strategies for churches, ministries, and God-ordained companies through leadership which He establishes. Don't have the Miriam syndrome and get out of position. It is very dangerous to operate in this manner. Heed the voice of spiritual authorities. Listen to the voice of spiritual fathers.

God is using Jericho as an opportunity to test the hearts of the Hebrews to see if they are going to suffer from the same problem as the previous generation. They suffered with the problem of pride, rebellion, questioning God-ordained authority, and running their mouths. Will this generation listen to the voice of a spiritual father or will they want to stone him like the previous generation? The previous generation was kept out of Canaan because they talked too much. The previous generation didn't enter into destiny because they didn't appreciate and honor spiritual authority. The next generation had to conquer the land by listening to the voice of spiritual authority and keeping their mouths shut. Think about it.

God Will Test You

Some have said that God does not test His people. God certainly does not tempt His people; we can see this is clearly stated in James 1:13. The place we become confused is by equating testing with temptation; these are two completely different things. God does not tempt us with evil. He does not entice us to do something that is wrong; however, God does test us.

A test is where options are presented to us and we have to make a choice. All we have to do is look at the Bible to see that God does just that; He tests us. That is exactly what God is doing at Jericho. It is God who tests our heart, not the enemy (1 Thessalonians 2:4). The children of Israel were tested. Spiritual fathers who came before us have been tested. I've been tested, and I promise you that you will be tested.

I find it incredible that Jericho is one of the places that Elijah and Elisha visit on that final journey. I promise you that Elisha was tested many times in the years that he served Elijah. I'm sure that Elijah said things of which Elisha did not like or agree. Elisha could have left, but he stayed. I'm sure Elijah asked Elisha to do things that he either didn't understand or simply didn't want to do. However, Elisha stayed, served, endured, and was faithful.

I have experienced this personally. Spiritual authority has said things to me that I didn't want to hear. Unfortunately, I haven't always passed the tests, and I had to take them again. You cannot progress to the next level of victory, the next level of calling, or the next level of anointing until you pass the test. All spiritual sons are tested. I pray that you are faithful and pass the test.

Passing the Test

What's really incredible about the instructions that Joshua gives the Israelites is that not one person is documented as opposing the directive of Joshua. There isn't one detractor; they all passed the test. They were obedient. They didn't question; they weren't skeptical. They were simply obedient. I have found that simple obedience is always the best policy. Earlier in this book I called it "the spirit of YES." The spirit of yes can be defined as simply doing what spiritual authority requests.

I've found something interesting about the tests that God administers to us. He doesn't give us any indicator that He is going to test us. God likes pop quizzes. When you were in school you may have had a teacher who gave you a pop quiz. Anyone can study and memorize when they know they have an upcoming exam. However, sometimes this is not an indicator of what a student has actually learned, but rather that they know how to prepare themselves for a test.

God isn't interested in your ability to prepare yourself to simply pass a test for the sake of passing a test. He wants to know how you are going to live, behave, respond, and conduct yourself. He wants to see what knowledge you possess without knowing a test is coming. When you live it and possess a working knowledge you can pass the test with no problem.

In school, I always found I had no problems passing the test on the material I really knew and understood. If you don't pass the test, God is gracious, merciful, and long-suffering; you will continue to learn and be given another opportunity to pass. However, I have found it much easier to live according to His purposes, learn as I grow, and pass the test the first time. Pass the test and continue into victory.

The Fulfilled Promise

And the LORD said: "I have surely seen the oppression of My people who are in Egypt, and have heard their cry because of their taskmasters, for I know their sorrows. So I have come down to deliver them out of the hand of the Egyptians, and to bring them up from that land to a good and large land, to a land flowing with milk and honey (Exodus 3:7-8).

God always fulfills His promises. Hallelujah! God promised that not only would He deliver His people from Egyptian bondage, but also bring them into Canaan. This is seen as they conquer Jericho. God will always see that His plan is accomplished. The question is, will you cooperate with His plan?

It is God's plan for the generation that exited Egypt to enter Canaan; however, that generation never tastes Canaan's honey. Why? It is because they repeatedly failed the test. They fail the test ten times (Numbers 14:22). They repeatedly complain; they repeatedly go against God's authority. They fail on every level. They earn an "F" on the test. Contrastingly, the next generation passes the test and enters into the promise God made decades ago to their fathers.

I believe that Jericho is representative of stepping into the big picture of the call and promise that God has given you. We talked about Bethel being the seedbed of destiny—the place where you receive the seed that will spring forth into the fullness of what God has for you.

Jericho is the place where you see your call begin to blossom. It is where destiny begins to bud in its earliest state. That is what happened for the Hebrews. They knew that the entire land had been given to them; it had been promised to them. Their parents told them about the "land that flows with milk and honey." They were very acquainted with the place that God had prepared for them. The first glimpse of seeing the promise become reality was conquering Jericho. Now, they were beginning to reclaim what had always been intended for them.

During his journey with Elijah, Elisha had an understanding of what God wanted him to do. He had experienced his "mantle moment." Elisha had his "Bethel seedbed encounter."

Sometime within Elisha's moments with Elijah, he began to see portions of the dream he had meditated on be realized in his life. The dream began to spring forth into reality.

In my own life, I am seeing things that I have dreamed begin to spring up. I'm seeing prophetic words that have been spoken over my life begin to come forth. This very book is one of those things. I have received prophetic words about writing books. Mentors, spiritual authority, and people I respect talked to me about writing books. Now I am here today seeing the fulfilled promise begin to spring forth.

I know that the promises which are becoming reality today are largely because I passed certain tests. Just like the children of Israel at Jericho, everything that stands in the way of our destiny falls flat when we pass the test. When the opposition falls flat it makes way for you to enter into victory and claim what God has for you.

The conquest of Jericho was not the end of obedience. It wasn't the last test and it wasn't the last conquest, but it was important. It was an incredible act of obedience. It was a huge test the children of Israel passed, and it was the first conquest on their way to claiming the rightful destiny that God had ordained for them.

Embrace Jericho

I encourage you to embrace the Jericho process. Be like the psalmist who said, "Examine me, O LORD, and prove me; Try my mind and my heart" (Psalm 26:2). He was asking God to test him. Don't dread the testing, rather embrace it. Celebrate the testing because on the other side of the passed test is victory. On the other side of the test is the promise fulfilled in your life. Embrace Jericho.

CHAPTER 12
THE DOUBLE PORTION: JORDAN

Then Elijah said to him, "Stay here, please, for the LORD has sent me on to the Jordan." But he said, "As the LORD lives, and as your soul lives, I will not leave you!" So the two of them went on. And fifty men of the sons of the prophets went and stood facing them at a distance, while the two of them stood by the Jordan. Now Elijah took his mantle, rolled it up, and struck the water; and it was divided this way and that, so that the two of them crossed over on dry ground. And so it was, when they had crossed over, that Elijah said to Elisha, "Ask! What may I do for you, before I am taken away from you?" Elisha said, "Please let a double portion of your spirit be upon me." So he said, "You have asked a hard thing. Nevertheless, if you see me when I am taken from you, it shall be so for you; but if not, it shall not be so." Then it happened, as they continued on and talked, that suddenly a chariot of fire appeared with horses of fire, and separated the two of them; and Elijah went up by a whirlwind into heaven.

And Elisha saw it, and he cried out, "My father, my father, the chariot of Israel and its horsemen!" So he saw him no more. And he took hold of his own clothes and tore them into two pieces. He also took up the mantle of Elijah that had fallen from him, and went back and stood by the bank of the Jordan. Then he took the mantle of Elijah that had fallen from him, and struck the water, and said, "Where is the LORD God of Elijah?" And when he also had struck the water, it was divided this way and that; and Elisha crossed over (2 Kings 2:6-14).

From Gilgal to Bethel. From Bethel to Jericho. From Jericho to Jordan. This is the end of the line. This is where it all ends, yet still continues. Everything in Elisha's life has pointed to this moment. This turning point is not only for Elisha, but for the sons of the prophets and the entire nation of Israel. One of the most incredible, miraculous, and supernatural things is about to happen at the Jordan River—the place of persistent faithfulness, higher realms, and the double portion.

The Faithful Son

There are many types of sons. There is the unfaithful son who starts strong, but doesn't endure. As we have already talked about, Demas is a perfect example of the unfaithful son. He started fast, but wasn't able to finish. Demas didn't endure. One thing I have learned about life and destiny is that it doesn't matter how you start, but how you finish. Anyone can start fast. The question is this: can you endure? Can you finish?

There is the impetuous son who is perfectly typified in the parable of the Prodigal Son. This is the person who wants their inheritance before it is time. This son starts faithful, demands their inheritance, but then squanders what they have received from their father. Why was it squandered? I believe the answer is simple. He had not completed his process as a son. As we would say, "He got the cart ahead of the horse." He had not gained the maturity needed to handle his inheritance properly. It wasn't that his inheritance was gained in an improper manner; he just wasn't ready to handle it yet.

The worst thing that can happen to us is to receive the double portion, to receive a mantle, to receive an inheritance, before we are ready. If we demand our inheritance before we have been through the process of sonship, the very thing that was intended to be a blessing to us and others who we encounter will destroy us.

There is also the usurping son. Absalom, the son of David, is a perfect example. He felt as if his father didn't handle a situation properly, so he took it upon himself to do what he thought should have been done. He ended up trying to make himself look good in the eyes of the people and led a revolt against his father, proclaiming himself as king. As you probably know, things didn't end well for Absalom.

While in battle, Absalom's hair became entangled in a tree (a picture that shows that pride will get you tangled and tied up) and was killed by one of David's men. Absalom was part of the royal line; he was a legitimate son. However, because he thought he could do a better job than his father, it cost him his life. Absalom was full of pride and was a usurping son.

145

Then of course there is the faithful son. This is the one we should all desire to be. We should all desire to look like the faithful son. Being the faithful son isn't always easy. Being the faithful son isn't always the most fun. Being the faithful son doesn't always seem to afford the most glorious opportunities. However, it is worth it to be the faithful son. What you receive in being the faithful son is greater than anything others may say that you sacrifice by being committed and loyal. Elisha lost oxen, a field, and a plow, but he was about to gain a double portion of the Spirit that was on Elijah. The double portion and wearing the mantle was much more valuable than anything Elisha lost.

Incredibly on his final journey with Elijah, Elisha is constantly being discouraged by everyone around him. They are constantly telling him, 'Your master is going to be taken from you' (2 Kings 2:5, *paraphrased*). Elisha tells them to shut their mouths. I believe part of the reason that Elisha said this was because he wanted to communicate the fact that as long as Elijah was there, he was going to serve him. Nothing was going to separate Elisha from Elijah. Elisha refused to leave; he refused to let anything get him off course. Elisha maintained his spiritual alignment with Elijah so that he could receive the double portion mantle. Elisha was faithful until the very end; he was persistently faithful.

Elisha was so faithful that he did things that Elijah thought were totally unnecessary. Elijah is trying to get Elisha to stop following him—to stop serving. I believe this may have been due to Elijah's humility. He possibly felt as if Elisha had done enough.

I have found that true spiritual fathers, true spiritual authority, do not live demanding to be served or feeling the need to be served. Every legitimate and true spiritual father in the faith whom I have had the privilege of encountering have been some of the most humble, down-to-earth people you will ever meet. I have actually seen them discourage others from serving them because they felt it was unnecessary; they didn't need to be served in that manner.

Likewise, a true spiritual son will continue to serve no matter if the spiritual father feels like it is unnecessary. The true son or daughter understands that in being faithful to spiritual authority, they are in fact being faithful to Father God. Nothing will stop them from serving godly authorities in their lives.

True spiritual sons, like Elisha and Timothy, have a quality that I like to call persistent faithfulness. They are tenacious. When we look at the conclusion of Elijah's earthly ministry, Elisha is the only one who follows him until the very end. The Bible tells us that fifty other sons of the prophets stand "at a distance" (2 Kings 2:7). These others could have been faithful to the end like Elisha; however, they simply chose a different level of relationship. They loved Elijah. They even served him as the sons of the prophet. The others simply made the choice not to serve at the same level as Elisha did. Elisha chose the life of persistent faithfulness.

Your level of faithfulness will determine the level which you receive. Elisha chose to be a persistently faithful son—not a fleeting son, nor a part-time son. He was not one who says, "As long as everything is good, I'm with you." He is fiercely faithful. When you are a son who lives in persistent faithfulness it doesn't matter how difficult it is, nor does it matter what others say. You are going to serve and be like Elisha who poured water on the hands of the man of God. True spiritual sons refuse to stop serving, they refuse to stop being faithful. Nothing other than persistent faithfulness is an option in the life of a true spiritual son.

If you want to walk in a double portion mantle, you have to operate in persistent faithfulness. When Elisha makes his request known to Elijah—when he tells him he wants the double portion—he is actually telling him that he wants the blessing of a son. He has shown his true sonship; he has persevered until the very end. He now desires the mantle that he wore for only a moment many years ago to now be his to wear as his own. Elijah had done a lot in his lifetime, yet there was more to be done. Elisha desires to continue the ministry that Elijah conducted. Elisha's faithfulness did not end when he left the earth; he continued to be faithful; he continued to honor Elijah by continuing the work to which Elijah had dedicated his life. Elisha continued the spiritual legacy of Elijah.

The double portion is not given for the purpose of making someone famous or great. The double portion that Elisha received was not simply so he could work more miracles than Elijah. The mantle wasn't so Elisha could be a "show-off." The double portion was so Elisha could continue to be a faithful son. The mantle ensured that Elisha could properly honor God by being His voice in the earth. It allowed Elisha to honor Elijah by following in his footsteps.

Elisha was a son who was persistently faithful. He served Elijah for years. He did the things that others may have despised and thought were beneath them. To position yourself for a double portion anointing, you must be persistently faithful. To be a good son you must be faithful until the very end.

Flow Down

Elisha's tenacious and persistent faithfulness had positioned him to receive. It is fascinating that the place where Elisha receives the double portion is Jordan. I don't believe this to be some sort of coincidence. Jordan is the same place that Joshua first leads the children of Israel after Moses has died. It was the place where Joshua picked up the mantle of Moses and will now be where Elisha picks up the mantle of Elijah. The name *Jordan* means to flow down. In the place whose name means to flow down, there is soon to be an anointing that flows down to Elisha. Anointing always flows down.

Psalm 133 refers to oil (anointing) being poured on the head of Aaron and running DOWN to his beard and eventually his garments. The oil—the anointing—flows down. If you want to receive an anointing, you have to get underneath it. So many men and women of great power and great anointing started by serving a man or woman of great power and great anointing. When you get under a head that is anointed the oil will eventually run down on you as long as you don't abandon your spot. You have to be persistently faithful for the oil to get to you. Don't get out of alignment. STAY FAITHFUL!

Going Higher

There is one major difference between Elijah giving Elisha a double portion and any other recorded instance of a father releasing a double portion blessing on a son. Abraham died after he released the double portion blessing. Isaac died after releasing the double portion blessing. Jacob died after releasing the double portion. Every father in history died after releasing the double portion. Elijah didn't die; he was simply called up to a higher place. Elijah went to a new level.

I think we see an incredible picture of a relationship between spiritual fathers and sons and daughters. In the natural, a father was on his deathbed when he released an inheritance—a double portion. This is not true of spiritual fathers. Spiritual fathers are called to higher levels of glory. As spiritual fathers move higher in the spirit, the mantle in which they operate falls to those who have been persistently faithful sons and daughters.

Elijah didn't die. The Bible says Elijah "went up." His assignment changed. Elijah was pulled up higher. Because Elijah was pulled up higher and Elisha was the spiritual son of Elijah, Elisha was also pulled up to a higher place. It was the place of void that was created by Elijah going higher. The role that Elijah had filled had to be continued by someone. Elisha was now to continue the work of Elijah. Elisha the servant was now the Prophet Elisha.

You don't have to wait for thirty years to receive a double portion or to receive a mantle. True spiritual fathers are constantly being pulled up to higher levels of glory, and as a result, they are constantly releasing mantles to faithful sons. God designed things to function and operate in this manner. It functions this way to enable us to go from glory to glory. God is establishing His Kingdom and work in the earth through the relationship between spiritual fathers and spiritual sons.

I am not satisfied with where I currently am. I am content and abound where I am, but nevertheless unsatisfied. I believe a spiritual son has some holy dissatisfaction. We should want to go higher and do more for the kingdom of God. We should desire to serve more and be a great blessing to others. I believe Elisha always wanted the mantle; he always wanted more. He wanted to go higher. As you are faithful and the spiritual authority in your life is pulled up higher, you will receive the mantle to continue in the level of influence and glory in which they have been operating. You will do what they have done and continue their work as God calls them to new things. The difference is that you will now be authorized to flow in that office with even more power. I want more.

The Double Portion

Elisha wastes no time when he receives the double portion. Why? It is because after receiving the double portion it wasn't the end of the journey, it was the beginning of a new one. Elisha immediately moves in his first recorded miracle. He strikes the waters in the same manner that Elijah had, and the waters part in the same manner that they did for Elijah. Elisha is now under the double portion anointing.

Elijah has fourteen recorded miracles in the Bible. Elijah caused rain to cease for three and a half years (1 Kings 17:1), being fed by ravens at the Brook Cherith (1 Kings 17:4), multiplying the barrel of meal and cruse of oil (1 Kings 17:14), resurrecting the widow of Zarephath's son (1 Kings 17:22), calling of fire from heaven on the altar and defeating the prophets of Baal (1 Kings 18:38), causing it to rain (1 Kings 18:45), prophesying that Ahab's lineage would be destroyed (1 Kings 21:22), prophesying that Jezebel would be eaten by dogs (1 Kings 21:23), prophesying that Ahaziah would die of his illness (2 Kings 1:4), calling fire from heaven upon fifty soldiers (2 Kings 1:10), calling fire from heaven upon the second group of fifty soldiers (2 Kings 1:12), parting of the Jordan (2 Kings 2:8), prophesying that Elisha should have a double portion of his spirit (2 Kings 2:10), being called up to heaven in a whirlwind (2 Kings 2:11).

Elisha on the other hand has twenty-eight recorded miracles in the Bible. Elisha causes the parting of the Jordan (2 Kings 2:14), healing of the waters (2 Kings 2:21), calling down she-bears to consume mockers (2 Kings 2:24), filling the valley with water (2 Kings 3:17), deceiving of the Moabites with the valley of blood (2 Kings 3:22), filling the vessels of oil (2 Kings 4:4), prophesying that the Shunammite woman would have a son (2 Kings 4:16), resurrecting the Shunammite's son (2 Kings 4:34), purifying a pot of stew (2 Kings 4:41), multiplying barley bread to feed one hundred men (2 Kings 4:43), healing of Naaman from leprosy (2 Kings 5:14), discerning of Gehazi's transgression (2 Kings 5:26), cursing Gehazi with leprosy (2 Kings 5:27), floating of the iron axe head (2 Kings 6:6), prophesying the Syrian battle plans (2 Kings 6:9), seeing the vision of the horses and chariots of fire (2 Kings 6:17), smiting the Syrian army with blindness (2 Kings 6:18), bringing restoration of sight to the Syrian army (2 Kings 6:20), prophesying the end of famine (2 Kings 7:1), prophesying the scoffing nobleman would see but not partake of abundance (2 Kings 7:2), deceiving the Syrians with the sound of chariots (2 Kings 7:6), prophesying the seven-year famine (2 Kings 8:1), prophesying Ben-Hadad's death (2 Kings 8:10), prophesying Hazael's cruelty to Israel (2 Kings 8:12), prophesying that Jehu would smite the house of Ahab (2 Kings 9:7), prophesying that Joash would defeat the Syrians at Aphek (2 Kings 13:17), prophesying that Joash would smite Syria three times but not destroy them (2 Kings 13:19), and resurrecting the man touched by his bones (2 Kings 13:21).

This wasn't a double portion of the spirit of Elijah in name only. This is the double portion in power and demonstration. Elisha literally performed double the miracles that Elijah did. The amazing thing to me is the similarity of the miracles. As you look closely and study the lives, ministry, and miracles of Elijah and Elisha, there are many similarities in what was accomplished during their ministries. Elisha just had it manifest more in quantity and in frequency than Elijah. It was as if the same spirit that was on Elijah was now on Elisha. That's because it was.

This isn't simply some sort of "buzz phrase" when we talk about someone receiving a double portion of the anointing or spirit of another that they have served under. It is the manifestation of the anointing that worked in a generation before working in the next generation, only in greater frequency and demonstration. This is the way God designed it to work; this is what Jesus taught. Jesus said that those who believed on Him would do the greater works (John 14:12). I don't believe Jesus was necessarily talking about accomplishing greater feats or greater miracles than He did. Jesus raised the dead, healed the sick, cast out devils, multiplied food, and ministered reconciliation. It doesn't get any better or more powerful than that. Jesus was talking about seeing more miracles in quantity. He was talking about a double portion. This has always been the heart of the Father God. His desire is for the next generation to accomplish more than the generation who came before them. It has always been His plan for the ceiling of one generation to become the floor from which the next generation begins.

Get Ready for the Double Portion

I believe that God wants to raise up a generation in the earth today who understand proper Kingdom order. They understand the seed life. They understand honor and obedience. They understand the importance of continuing legacy. They understand synergy. They understand and embrace Gilgal: covenant and cutting. They understand and embrace Bethel: encounter, dream, and the dying of self. They understand and embrace Jericho: the test and fulfilled dream. Lastly, this generation has properly positioned themselves for Jordan: the double portion.

I can see in my spirit an army of men and women—of sons and daughters—who have been faithful to the process. This company of people have died to themselves and is so full of the power of God that they will be spoken of in the same manner as the Church of Acts. It will be said of them, "These are those who turned the world upside down" (Acts 17:6). I see a generation that sees God in a place of priority in every nation of the earth. I see a generation that can't go anywhere without miracles breaking out. I see a generation that can and will win the world for Jesus.

This will transpire and come through the hands of persistently faithful spiritual sons and daughters who have endured the process and received the double portion anointing from spiritual fathers to whom they have submitted their lives.

Be faithful. Receive the double portion. Change the world.

AFTERWORD

By Robert Gay
Senior Pastor, High Praise Worship Center

In this book *Sonship*, Joshua Gay has clearly outlined the principles that are needed for spiritual maturity in the life of a believer. Through both precept and example, he has marvelously presented how Christians can travel from a place of being babes in Christ to young men who are strong and eventually to fathers in the faith. There are many principles expounded upon that will produce good fruit within the life of any individual who will choose to enact this teaching. God is not a respecter of persons and His Word will work for anyone who will practice it.

There are many people today who desire the double portion, but there are fewer who are willing to travel down the path that arrives at that destination. There are many who have cried out for the Father God to teach them His ways, yet when the instruction comes through a spiritual father seeking to bring admonition and correction, they reject it. There are many who have prayed and sought the Lord for a greater anointing, yet in the midst of the process that produces the oil, they have aborted their journey.

Joshua has fluently revealed how the anointing is produced within the lives of God's people. He has used both biblical and personal example to bring these things to light. As his father, I can attest that he has lived the words within this book. This teaching is not merely a revelation that he possesses. Rather, it is a lifestyle that he has lived and practiced. This has resulted in God's blessing manifested within his life.

The reality is that we live in an age of instant gratification. We want something and we want it NOW! The thought of a process being required for the fulfillment of one's desire is difficult for some to understand and grasp. However, there is a process for everything within the kingdom of God. Everything operates on the principle of seed and that seed being planted. Joshua has brought a powerful understanding of the process of a seed from the time that is planted until the time of full maturity and fruit bearing. We are like seed that must be planted so that we can become those trees that produce abundant fruit.

For many, this principle of the seed is foreign since we have been taught that all we need to do for a double portion anointing is merely go through a prayer line or send an offering to a television ministry. My friend, not only is that unscriptural, but IT DOESN'T WORK! I've seen people do all sorts of things in an attempt to take spiritual shortcuts. However, that is not the biblical pattern that God has established. God has a process for everything He does within our lives.

Joshua has shown how that the one who will yield to God's divine growth process will see their ultimate destiny within the kingdom of God fulfilled. The person who will practice the principles of sonship that are outlined in this book will see God perform marvelous things in their lives. As they allow the journey to the double portion anointing transpire within their lives, they will witness growth and maturity that will position them for God's best and greatest blessings.

In some circles, words like *submission* and *obedience* have become bywords. However, these are the things that are necessary for any individual to travel down the path of maturity and sonship. These are foundations for true spiritual growth that will enable one to transition from a spiritual baby to a spiritual man or woman of God. These are the marks that distinguish the "men from the boys." These are the characteristics that are readily observed in mature sons and are missing in the rebellious and obstinate.

When I first read this book I experienced a range of emotions. I was very gratified that my son had written a book that expressed what I believe to be the wisdom of God. At times I wept with tears of thankfulness that my son had become a man that could articulate the heart of the Father. There were also emotions of joy that this understanding could now be had by all those who would read this book.

Could it be that the Father God feels the same way when He sees us mature into full grown sons and daughters? Could it be that He is filled with joy knowing that we have moved beyond "spiritual babyhood"? Could it be that He is gratified when we begin to express His wisdom as opposed to immature behavior? Could it be that there is joyous celebration when we begin to express His heart from a place of maturity as sons and daughters? I believe so.

I trust that this book is not merely another "read" for you. I trust that there has been an impartation that will make a difference in your life. The principles found within this book will profoundly change your life if you will enact them. I encourage you to submit to God's process and become that mature son or daughter of God. Your journey of sonship to the double portion will be worth it. Take that journey!

ABOUT THE AUTHOR

Joshua Gay serves as Executive Pastor of High Praise Worship Center in Panama City, Florida. Joshua began serving in ministry at a young age and has dedicated his life to promoting and propagating the Gospel of Jesus Christ. Joshua's zeal for the Word and his passion for the presence of God have touched the hearts of those both young and old. His teachings are illuminating and revelatory bringing encouragement to all who hear them. Joshua and his wife, Miranda, have two children, Josiah and Hannalee.

CONNECT WITH JOSHUA GAY

 FACEBOOK.COM/PASTORJOSHUAGAY   TWITTER.COM/PASTORJOSHUAGAY

for more information on available products
or ministry scheduling, contact us at:
www.PastorJoshuaGay.com

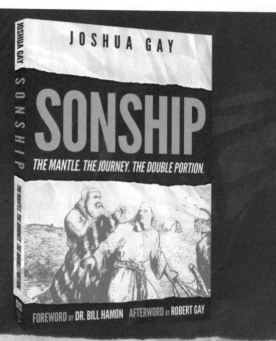

SONSHIP
THE MANTLE. THE JOURNEY. THE DOUBLE PORTION.

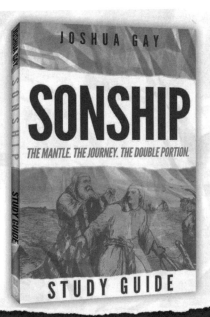

Next Level: Raising The Standard Of Grace
Pastor Robert Gay

In this book, Robert is sounding a trumpet call from heaven, engaging the reader to see the Ten Commandments afresh from the empowering view of God's Grace. Robert clearly and biblically explains how Grace takes the Ten Commandments to the *Next Level* and empowers us to live godly, holy lives above sin. There is no limit to the success, prosperity & blessings that will surround you when you apply the principles of *Next Level*.

Conquering King
High Praise Worship

This album is packed full of powerful and anointed praise and worship that will usher you into the presence of the Lord. This album features songs such as: *God Is Fighting, I Believe, Great Is The Lord, Awesome God, I Will Worship, Jehovah Jireh, Mercy Rain, We Are Overcomers, Conquering King* and more.

for more info or to order any of these porducts visit our online store at
WWW.HIGHPRAISEPC.COM/ONLINE-STORE

Silencing The Enemy With Praise
Pastor Robert Gay

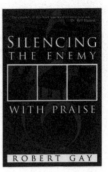

Praise and worship are more than words and music says author Pastor Robert Gay. Praise is a weapon of warfare. God will fight for you as you praise the greatness of His name.

"The contents of this book can revolutionize your life...It brings new understanding about the power of praise and worship."
-Dr. Bill Hamon

Planted
Pastor Robert Gay

Robert Gay confronts common "church issues" head on. He teaches with clarity and compassion that God is the Master Gardener who lovingly tends to every individual planted in His garden. You will find out how God wants to plant you so that you will flourish and grow and become everything He wants you to be.

"Every Pastor will appreciate this book...every saint of God should read this book..." - Dr. Bill Hamon

Best Of Robert Gay
Pastor Robert Gay

This compilation album represents some of Robert's most impactful songs that have touched the body of Christ throughout the world. This cd is packed full with 19 tracks that include powerful songs such as Mighty Man of War, Lord Sabaoth, On Bended Knee, Holy is Your Name, One Voice, No Other Name and much more!

HIGH PRAISE
worship center

EQUIPPING BELIEVERS, BUILDING FAMILIES, AND FURTHERING THE KINGDOM OF GOD

FOR MORE INFORMATION ABOUT BOOKS, MUSIC, AND TEACHING CDS BY ROBERT GAY, VISIT US AT: WWW.HIGHPRAISEPC.COM

CONNECT WITH US

FACEBOOK.COM/HIGHPRAISEPC   TWITTER.COM/HIGHPRAISEPC   YOUTUBE.COM/HIGHPRAISEPC

HIGH PRAISE WORSHIP CENTER
7124 E. HWY. 22
PANAMA CITY, FL 32404

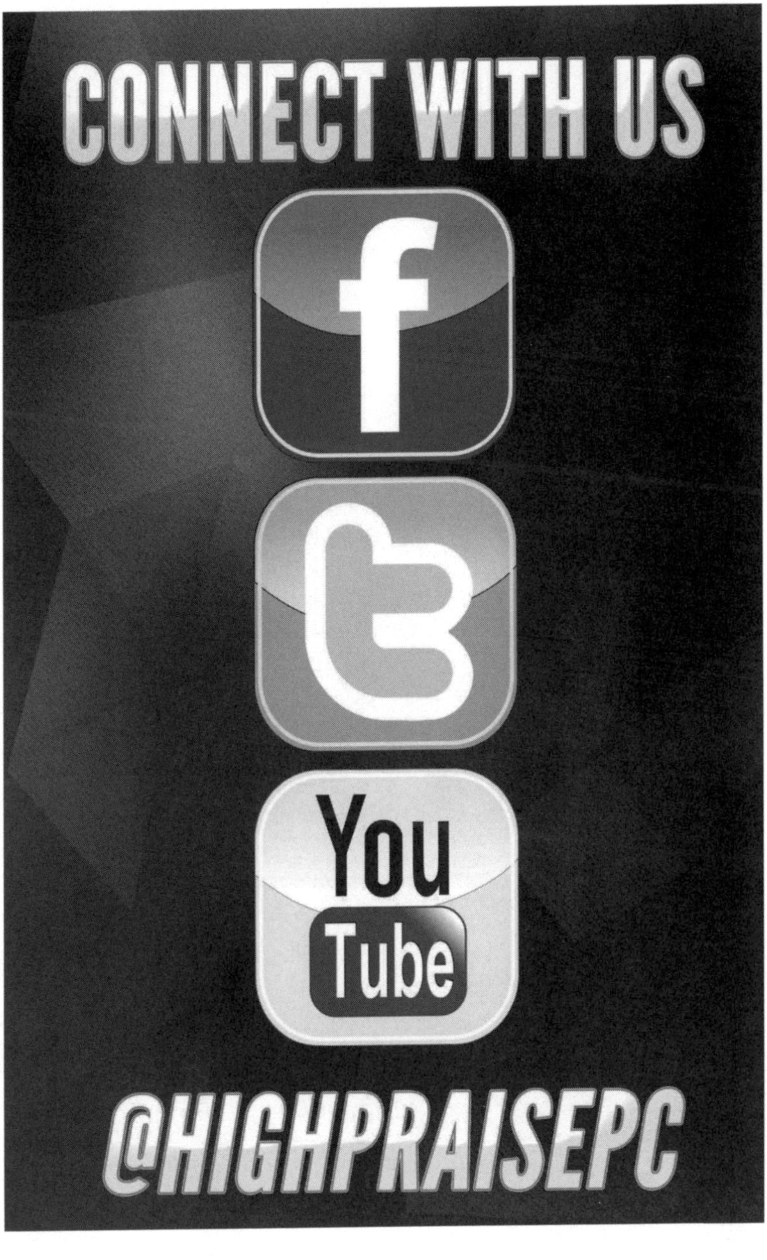
CONNECT WITH US
You
Tube
@HIGHPRAISEPC